TRANSFORM ONLINE TEACHING

EXPERT STRATEGIES
AND
ESSENTIAL RESOURCES
EVERY EDUCATOR NEEDS

BY

DR. BRUCE A. JOHNSON

Table of Contents

About the Author

Dr. Bruce A. Johnson is an academic leader and innovative educator with experience in higher education as Chief Academic Officer and Dean, along with work as an online instructor and college professor. Dr. J's background also includes work as a corporate trainer and manager of a corporate training development.

Dr. Johnson has developed expertise in his career with academic program development, curriculum development, adult education, distance learning, online teaching, faculty development, career coaching, resume writing, and organizational learning. Dr. J completed a Master in Business Administration (MBA) and a PhD in Education, with a specialization in Postsecondary and Adult Education.

Introduction

Many educators who begin to teach online believe they can make the transition easily from teaching in a traditional college classroom to an online classroom. What they don't realize, if they don't seek out resources to help them learn how to teach in a virtual environment, is that they are putting themselves and their class at a disadvantage. The reason why is due to the significant difference between classroom teaching and online teaching. It isn't because the principles of adult learning have changed, or the needs of adult students have changed, rather it is due to the change in the format of learning.

Educators who have taught in a traditional classroom are often surprised to discover that online teaching requires a different instructional strategy, and even the use of a different set of skills, when they first become acquainted with a virtual learning environment. The transition can be fairly easy for some educators to make, and much more challenging for others, especially if they have become accustomed to teaching in a particular manner and have not needed to change (or they have not been willing to change) their approach ^to classroom instruction.

Online teaching is not just about learning how to set up an online classroom and adding learning resources; it is a matter of how the class is taught and the manner of instruction used. To become an effective online instructor there must be thought given as to how the technological tools will be used, how to translate traditional communication into digital communication, and how to evolve from an instructor who stands in front of a class and directs the flow of conversations and interactions to someone who can facilitate and guide the learning process, while keeping students interested and engaged in the course.

Learning to teach online requires having an open mind and a willingness to learn, along with making an allowance for the time needed to implement new methods - while monitoring instructional effectiveness until excellence is achieved.

Pedagogy versus Andragogy

There are two primary principles that are relevant for the field of education, pedagogy and andragogy. The principle of andragogy is meant to address teaching adults and it is generally based upon the premise that adults are self-motivated as students who have specific needs and want to be involved in an active learning environment. They also have existing knowledge and experience that needs to be acknowledged and leveraged in some manner by their instructors.

This is in contrast to the principle of pedagogy or teaching children, which is a teacher-centered environment where the students are told what to learn and how to learn. These students are expected to be passive participants in the learning process, or blank slates who are awaiting knowledge from the teacher.

A primary challenge for college instructors who want to apply the principle of andragogy to their teaching practice is that the traditional methods of teaching adults in a college or university environment is still aligned with the principle of pedagogy to some degree. In other words, the teacher in a traditional classroom delivers a lecture, directs what students must learn, and measures their progress through a midterm and final exam. This leaves them with little flexibility to address the needs of adult students as outlined by the principle of andragogy.

What educators find is that the nature of the online classroom requires them to find new methods of teaching and now they have more flexibility to add in a variety of techniques that better address what adult students need.

Verbal versus Written Instruction

An aspect of online teaching that is challenging for traditional instructors at first involves making a transition from verbally presenting their lectures to posting written messages as a new form of lecture. When an instructor prepares their class lecture they either create notes or speak from memory, without consideration given to the mechanics of those notes or what is going to be spoken as they are the only one who will be reading those notes.

When an instructor teaches online the mechanics matter more than ever as that is the primary form of communication and those words now represent the instructor. This requires a change in thought process and approach to the development of instructional materials and communication.

The following is a sample of what might be spoken during a class lecture and how it could be written if there was no consideration made for the mechanics of the lecture: hello class. Today were going to talk about managing employees and we have alot to cover. A manager must learn to have patient with there employees which is something i learned in my career. Ive also learned there is a difference between leading and managing as a manger i worked to develop employees based on their strengths...

As you can see from this sample there are numerous errors, and these are common errors among adult students who are used to verbal rather than written communication. This is not to imply that instructors are not proficient in writing, rather it is meant to illustrate a shift in thinking that is required now. For example, if an instructor put this lecture into an online classroom in this manner there would be a negative perception held by students about that instructor.

For those instructors who are proficient writers and have well-developed academic skills of their own, making this transition would not be challenging. But there are also instructors who have not been required to submit written lectures or participate in professional development activities that require some form of writing activity, and this presents a challenge for teaching online. Now all aspects of written communication matter and it takes time and practice to learn to use proper mechanics.

Telling versus Showing

The issue of proper writing, along with the development of academic skills for instructors, also applies to another important aspect of online teaching - working with information that has been obtained from sources, whether these sources were obtained from online websites or from an online library database. Traditional classroom instructors are generally well-aware of copyright restrictions when utilizing sources in class but this extends further with online teaching.

During a classroom lecture an instructor may tell students about an article that was recently reviewed and that would likely be sufficient for that particular classroom environment. However, there is a notable difference between talking about sources and writing a classroom post, one that incorporates information from sources in some manner - whether quoted directly or paraphrased indirectly.

For example, an online instructor would not be advised to post a written message that states the following: In a Forbes article there was advice given about managing employees that indicated "employees need to be taught about empowerment". Or it might be written without the quotation marks and just stated directly in that same sentence.

For both of these examples the sources were not properly acknowledged with correctly formatted in-text citations and that would be an example of accidental plagiarism. In a traditional class an instructor may not need to explain the use of sources from the perspective of properly formatting in-text citations and a reference list, especially if they don't require students to write papers that must include the support of additional research.

This is different when posting information in an online class as proper citations must be used and formatting guidelines followed to prevent copyright infringement and plagiarism. Properly formatted posts also serve as a model for students to follow and it teaches them how to properly work with sources. There may be a steep learning curve for instructors, especially those who have not been required to learn a specific formatting style, and it is important to find and utilize resources that will help improve areas of needed development.

Expertise versus Open-Mindedness

Over time, classroom instructors become well-versed in teaching their subject matter and that expertise serves them well. If they receive positive class reviews and have no need to develop their teaching skills further, it can establish a mindset of being an expert instructor. For those instructors, learning to teach online challenges this mindset as those same methods of teaching will not automatically translate into a virtual classroom environment.

Even the general format and structure of the class has changed as lectures are no longer delivered on specified class meetings and instead, students have access to their class virtually every day of the week. Now instructors are required to be available for more than their traditional scheduled meetings. What this new method of teaching requires is being open-minded and that can be challenging if instructors believe they already are the expert or authority in teaching, which they very well may be for a traditional class.

Rigidity versus Adaptability

The attitude held about learning to teach online influences and ultimately determines how effective the instructor will be as they begin to work in this type of environment. This attitude also includes being comfortable with technology and a willingness to try new technological tools. An instructor who is new to online teaching can either become willing to learn this method of instruction, or resist and allow frustration to set in.

As a result of the demands of adapting to a virtual class, some instructors develop a rigid mindset and decide they do not want to learn new instructional methods or strategies. Becoming an online instructor requires flexibility and adaptability. I decided when I became an online instructor that I would remain open to learning new instructional methods and technological tools, and that has served me well ever since that time.

Facilitator versus Educator

Another reason why online teaching is challenging at first for traditional instructors is that they are no longer at the front and center of every class, from the perspective of their visual presence. Some schools use the word facilitator to describe the work of an online instructor and while it may seem that a facilitator is someone who is sitting on the sidelines their role is much more important.

An online instructor must be highly engaged and involved in their class if they are going to keep students interested in the class. Their role as an educator hasn't changed but the format has and that requires the development of new instructional strategies.

Online teaching is different than classroom teaching and it is more than the use of a technology-enabled classroom that creates those differences. Becoming a successful online instructor involves more than knowing how to set up a class and utilize the technological tools that are available.

This form of teaching requires the development of an active virtual presence, learning to communicate effectively through written posts and messages, and nurturing productive working relationships with students you cannot see. Most instructors can successfully develop new methods of teaching and communicating in this environment if they are willing to learn and adapt their existing instructional methods.

Transforming Online Teaching

The purpose of this book is to provide you with strategies and resources that I have learned and implemented throughout my career, working as an online educator, faculty development specialist, and Chief Academic Officer. Over the past ten years I have interviewed, hired, trained, mentored, and reviewed the performance of hundreds of online faculty members.

This book was written to provide you with a professional development opportunity. You can choose to read it from beginning to end, or you can choose a chapter to review at the start of each course you are assigned to teach. You may also find it useful to review specific topics of interest after you have conducted a self-assessment at the end of a class.

My hope is that you are inspired as an online educator to develop engaging instructional practices, connect with students in a meaningful manner, and perform your very best.

Dr. Bruce A. Johnson
September 2016

CHAPTER 1.
BECOMING VISIBLE IN A VIRTUAL CLASS

For anyone who is interested in online teaching, whether as a full time career or for part time adjunct work, it may seem fairly simple to get started, especially when the classroom and the curriculum has been pre-developed for you. However, there are many important aspects of online teaching that need development and are applicable whether you are teaching full time or not. This includes **what** you teach and **how** you teach.

For the aspect of **what** you teach it is addressed through the course syllabus and course materials provided, and enhanced by your background and professional experience. The perspective concerning **how** you teach is a matter of developing your instructional techniques and strategies. The **how** you teach is the purpose of this book, to provide new online instructors (as well as seasoned instructors) with techniques and strategies that can help increase effectiveness with online teaching.

New instructors usually experience a significant learning curve as they begin to work towards meeting the required facilitation duties, especially as they learn the specifics of the contractual duties. Those instructors who have received some type of onboarding or new faculty training may be better prepared to adapt to a technologically-enabled classroom environment.

However, from my experience with online faculty development that initial training is typically focused on navigating through the classroom and utilizing tools that are available with the school's learning management system. For many instructors, learning the technological side of online teaching can become overwhelming and overshadow the development of personal instructional strategies at first, which means that meeting instructional duties takes preference over developing instructional strategies.

The first aspect of online teaching that an instructor needs to be concerned about, even for instructors who have already taught online classes, is their instructional presence. An instructor's presence in a class, for any type of classroom environment, is essential for the development of a productive learning experience. The level of involvement by the instructor influences all aspects of student learning, including how interested and engaged students will be in the class, their level of motivation, and how well they perform.

However, there is a difference between being present in a traditional class and an online class. For a traditional college classroom an instructor is present during scheduled class meetings and that changes with an online class as this type of class is open virtually every day of the week and it is possible that students can be present at any time.

It is important as you begin to develop your online teaching practice that you also consider the possible perspective of your students and what an instructional presence might mean to them. Students develop perceptions about the instructor and the school based upon how the course is designed and more importantly, the level of involvement by their instructor. Students who attend a traditional classroom have the immediate benefit of visually observing the instructor and their involvement in the class, which provides important guidance and feedback about the learning process. The nature of those visual observations change with an online classroom environment and students look for other indicators to let them know their instructor is actively present and engaged in the class.

Online teaching is viewed by some instructors as a function that must be managed, while most see the true potential it holds and that it is a process they must nurture over time. If instructors are going to create conditions that are conducive to learning they must do more than manage the functions of a class; they must be active, present, responsive, and available for students.

A challenge that must be addressed is developing a virtual form of social interactions while never being able to actually meet the students face-to-face. As a result of the absence of direct contact and established weekly class meetings when all students must be in attendance, online instructors need to become accessible to students in some manner rather than being viewed as an anonymous person who may seem distant from them.

Through the development of engaging instructional methods, and the use of techniques that increases their visibility in the class, instructors are able to become a "real" person to students, at least from a perceptual basis. This creates a connection with students and helps develop productive working relationships.

The Need for a Strong Virtual Presence

Since an instructor's presence is a critical component of any classroom environment, establishing a virtual presence needs to be one of the first instructional strategies that are implemented, which begins to address **how** you teach. Within a traditional classroom the instructor is physically present and it is that presence that maintains social interactions, guides discussions, and builds relationships with the students. These direct interactions are absent from the online classroom environment; however, it is still possible for an instructor to develop a strong virtual presence through the use of indirect interactions.

Any instructor who wants to work in a virtual environment has an ability to develop a strong virtual presence by adapting their traditional facilitation methods. For instructors who are used to teaching in a physical classroom they may find that new techniques are now required. Without the physical presence of an instructor, online facilitation occurs through the processes such as communication, feedback, and relationship-building.

Within a technology-enabled learning platform an instructional presence is possible when instructors are active in class discussions and they are quickly responding to students' questions and the overall classroom conditions. Students develop perceptions about the class, the process of learning, and the school based upon their classroom interactions and they are likely to find it reassuring to know that their instructor is dedicated to their progress and overall development.

An important component of an effective online presence is the instructor's availability. In order for students to feel connected to the classroom environment they need to know that their instructor is readily available on a regular basis. This means conducting more than an occasional check-in with the class; a strong instructional presence must include the instructor's active and ongoing engagement and participation.

An effective method of demonstrating availability is answering questions and emails within a timely manner. Some adjuncts utilize instant messaging as a means of being available for their students. Overall, being actively engaged and present in the class results in a positive experience for the instructor and the students, and promotes a productive learning environment.

A Change in the Format of Learning

Within a traditional classroom an instructor provides the direct delivery of information, while nurturing face-to-face student interactions and participating in live, synchronous class discussions. It also means this classroom environment is still teacher-led, which is similar to the teaching approach that is used in primary education. The benefit of this approach is that an instructor is able to gauge the level of student engagement, and even their level of interest and motivation, and adapt the instructional methods used based upon what is physically observed. Another benefit is that meeting in class allows them to reach out to students when there are performance issues to address.

The online classroom has changed this traditional format of learning. An online classroom environment can become mechanical in nature or nurtured as a meaningful learning experience for students, which requires an instructor to develop a new type of classroom presence, relying upon indirect methods of presenting information and participating in asynchronous classroom discussions. The online instructor is also responsible for guiding and assisting the students as they work in this technologically-enabled environment, changing the nature of instruction from a teacher who transmits knowledge (teacher-led) to an instructor who facilitates the learning process (student-centered). In a student-centered environment it is possible that an online instructor can still guide the development of classroom relationships and interactions by creating conditions that are conducive to and supportive of productive exchanges.

For the online instructor, relationships between students and the instructor are primarily based upon written communication without the benefit of verbal communication or follow up, unless the instructor makes that option available. Words now form the basis of communication and interactions occur more frequently as the online classroom is always available. A common challenge for instructors who are teaching in an online classroom is modeling active engagement so that students are motivated to also be actively present. The reason why this is challenging is that a virtual classroom is always "open" and students expect to "see" their instructor in the classroom on a regular basis. Most online schools also expect instructors to be available for more than one scheduled class meeting and establish a minimum number of days that they are expected to be present in the classroom, usually associated with participation in class discussions.

The reason why there is mandatory involvement is that an instructional presence becomes evident to students when the instructor is active in the discussions and proactively responding to class conditions. While the format of the learning environment may have changed with an online platform the students' need for one-on-one interactions does not change. Scheduling planned participation within the discussions, and on specific days of the week, is a method instructors utilize to demonstrate their active role in the process of learning. Through frequent postings that begin early in the class week, along with the use of questions that engage students further in the discussion, instructors are able to replicate - to some extent - the interactive nature of the traditional classroom.

Instructors can ask directed questions and help encourage students to be responsive to the ongoing conversations, while remaining focused on the required topics. However, the development of substantive participation does require an additional investment of time, especially for adjunct instructors who are balancing numerous responsibilities. A common challenge for instructors who teach in this environment then becomes their ability to model active engagement in the class so that their students are also motivated to be actively engaged, which is why instructor participation must be considered an instructional strategy that needs to be cultivated, over time and through ongoing practice.

How to Become Visible in a Virtual Classroom

The online classroom has changed the format of traditional learning but not the basic principles of adult education. Written words now form the basis of communication and interactions occur more frequently as the online classroom is almost always accessible and available, and the learning process now relies on digital interactions in a virtually created environment. There are steps that any online instructor can implement to create a strong virtual classroom presence.

#1. Introduce Yourself to Students

Most online classes that I've taught had a requirement during the first week for introductions, both on the part of the instructor and the students. This presents an opportunity to become a "real" person to students by sharing something from your background, along with your professional experience. Some instructors believe their introductory post should be casual in nature and others maintain strict professionalism.

My approach is to try to find a balance in between so that my introduction does not appear to be a written resume. I share highlights of my academic accomplishments, areas of ongoing research, and something about a personal hobby, along with social media links that are professional in nature so students can learn more about my background and connect with me. This includes websites such as Twitter or LinkedIn. I also find it helpful to share a professional photo, which helps to further humanize the learning experience.

#2. Utilize the Full Potential of Class Announcements

Most online schools provide courses that are pre-developed for instructors and that means they do not have to set up the discussion forums, lessons, gradebook, and other required technological tools. However, one of the elements that instructors generally do have control over is the use of class announcements. This is another opportunity to demonstrate to your students that you are actively involved in the class as you can share tips, resources, and strategies based upon what you've observed in the class and the needs of your students.

As an example, when I have observed students struggling with class participation, I will post an update with suggestions for developing substantive posts. What I have also found useful is to include a photo at the top of the announcements, something that is related to the subject matter, as this helps to create visual interest in the message. And if you have the option to generate an email version of the announcement, this is an effective method of sending the information directly to your students.

#3. Begin Participation Early in the Class Week

Based upon my work with online faculty development, some instructors look forward to class discussions and others see it as a tedious task where students are posting the same type of responses, making it difficult to engage them in an interesting discussion. It is really up to the instructor to set the tone and establish a model of participation for students to follow. I begin posting my responses early in the week, as soon as students start posting. I will have already provided tips and tools for developing discussion posts and then I will use each response, no matter how well or poorly it was developed, as a springboard for engaging students in the topic. Typically, I'll acknowledge something the student has written, build from it with my experience, expertise, and/or information from the course materials, and then conclude with a thoughtful question. This can take student responses that seem similar in nature and transform them into something meaningful.

#4. Establish Multiple Methods of Availability

The usual method of contact that instructors offer is email, along with a phone number for pressing issues or questions. Some instructors also utilize instant messaging and/or Skype as a means of being available for their students during specified times. Some learning management systems have a built-in tool such as Adobe Connect for contact. I offer students these options and I also establish weekly office hours at a time when students are most likely to be online and working.

It is easy to establish office hours while you plan to work on feedback and you'll find it helpful to schedule more than one session during the class week, especially towards the end of the week when students are working towards completion of the learning activities. I make it a practice to check for and answer emails frequently, most days of the week. The reason why is that I remember what it was like as an online student to wait for an answer so I make certain my students don't have to wait long for a reply.

#5. Demonstrate Your Responsiveness to Students

When you are actively involved in your class, managing it effectively, and addressing the developmental needs of your students in a proactive and thoughtful manner, you are demonstrating your responsiveness to them. Being responsive means that you care about the academic well-being of your students and they will quickly learn that they can count on you to help them when needed, even if you aren't online and in the classroom every time they are - especially if they know when you are scheduled to be available and that you respond to their questions or concerns within a fairly reasonable time.

Interactions Matter More Than Ever

You must be readily available and accessible for your students based upon whatever conditions you can establish. You can establish a working schedule and communicate your availability to your students. It is helpful for them to also know the general time frame you have planned to answer emails and their questions, and when you may be available for direct contact through office hours, chat, phone, or other options that you have established for them.

Your active presence is also needed to assure students you are in control of the class and aware of the conditions of this virtual environment. Your involvement also has another effect, you are humanizing the learning experience for students and that will help them feel a sense of belonging to a community of real people rather than a collection of student identification numbers.

The interactions you have with students are most effective when you have developed a strong virtual presence, one that is focused on the needs of your students, and creates positive feelings for them about being involved in their class. Being actively present in the class results in a positive experience overall for both the instructor and the students, and promotes a highly productive learning environment. An instructional presence needs to be planned, scheduled, and occur frequently throughout the week. My recommendation to instructors is don't be present because you have to but instead because you want to, as a means of showing that you truly care about your students.

Establishing a Positive Online Instructional Image

As an online instructor do you consider the virtual or perceptual image you have established with your students? Do you consider the image you portray and how this image is developed throughout the course? If so, how do you manage your image?

An online instructor is represented with every classroom post and every message sent to the students. A virtual image is developed through students' perceptual processing and is influenced by the perceived tone of the instructor's messages, the word choice utilized, and mechanics of everything that has been written. Development of a positive online instructional image is necessary as it has a direct influence on working relationships, which are built through one interaction at a time, and how receptive students are to their instructor's guidance, feedback, and support.

Within an online classroom, students typically become acquainted with their instructor when they read the introduction or biography posted. This presents an opportunity for the instructor to share highlights of their background, which includes their experience and education, as a means of creating an image of being knowledgeable, personable, and a "real" person to the students. The importance of the classroom introduction should not be overlooked as a brief response may be perceived as a lack of caring when it needs to promote a sense of community. This introduction can be enhanced by inviting students to professional social networking platforms such as Twitter or LinkedIn. Instructors should be cautious about utilizing Facebook, if their profile reveals personal information that would have a negative impact on their virtual instructional presence.

Instructors have another opportunity to enhance their virtual image through messages posted in the classroom. For online lectures and instructional participation postings instructors can demonstrate their subject matter expertise, which has a direct impact on their credibility. Students also develop a sense of who their instructor is when they review the feedback provided.

Your image as an instructor may be that of someone who truly cares about their students' development or someone who demands compliance with their expectations. The challenge when creating these messages is to utilize wording that is professional but does not talk up to or down to students. In addition, the wording should be engaging and utilized as a means of encouraging productive communication, if the goal is to create a responsive presence. Some instructors prefer a direct approach to classroom facilitation and choose to establish an authoritative presence.

The online classroom environment requires an instructional approach that bridges the gap between technology and students. Students' engagement in the class is often influenced by their perception of the classroom environment, which is directly affected by the instructor's virtual presence. Should an instructor care about their image? The answer is yes, if the instructor wants to develop meaningful interactions and effective communication. A positive online instructional image helps to build a sense of working together and can increase students' acceptance of feedback, coaching, and guidance provided. Instructors can develop a strong image by paying attention to their communication, their postings, and their interactions. It can be further enhanced through the use of professional social networking. Instructors develop facilitation techniques that are designed to influence the process of learning and students will respond favorably if they have a positive overall perception of their instructor and the instructor's abilities.

End of Chapter Check-In

What Have You Learned?

What Are Your Strengths?

What Are Your Developmental Areas?

What Will You Apply to Your Teaching Practice?

CHAPTER 2.
WORKING WITH ONLINE STUDENTS

Getting to Know Online Students Requires Effort

In a traditional college class, instructors will likely have a fairly predictable group of students who can be visually assessed, even though these visual perceptions may not always be accurate. This is different for a class of online students as there can be a greater variety of backgrounds and experiences, which is why the traditional definition of a college student is no longer applicable. That's why the phrase "non-traditional students" has been used to describe online students as it represents a group of students who have different needs than traditional college students. It becomes imperative for online instructors to learn about their students during the course if they are going to be able to assist them and support their ongoing progress.

Within an online class it is possible to have students with learning disabilities, physical disabilities, and mental impairments, along with other forms of physical and mental challenges. There is a saying that you should not judge a book by its cover and with online students there is no visible cover to assess. Even the phrases used to describe learning within a technologically enabled environment are not very encouraging. For example, "online learning" sounds mechanical and "distance learning" sounds far away. But at the heart of teaching in any environment, especially for the online classroom, is the instructor and student relationship. If that relationship can be developed, even during a limited class time, it will help to improve student success and retention.

Online Students and Their Identity

At first an online instructor may view their students as a single type because they all appear to be the same when represented by a printed name or number. Some learning management system platforms now allow students and instructors to upload a photo and attach it to their profile as a means of personalizing classroom posts. From the students' perspective there are still some who are reluctant to share any personal information, some who share too many details, and others who want to hide behind their anonymity. When a student believes they are anonymous they are more likely to express their thoughts freely and seemingly without any consequences. In my experience some students have even felt empowered from their perception of freedom and talk without a filter to other students and their instructors.

Behind every name listed in the classroom is someone who wants to complete a goal but they may not be able to express themselves effectively, especially if they have identity issues. An identity is developed as a result of their internalized self-beliefs, which have been maintained over time and do not change easily or quickly. When students participate in their class those prior problems and challenges related to their identity still exist, including a negative self-image. An instructor can help them discover their authentic self through the use of supportive communication, interactions, and feedback.

Overcoming Anonymity

Students cannot be forced to interact with their instructors beyond what is required of them, such as involvement in the discussion board. However, through the development of a strong working relationship it may be possible to gain their cooperation. Sometimes a student's reluctance is the result of their perceptions or prior negative experiences, and that requires extra effort on the part of their instructor to change that mindset. Students can either be coaxed out of anonymity or they may retreat further into their shell. There are steps you can take to get to know your students and encourage the development of their online personality. For example, you can utilize different options for posting their introduction, including the use of a recorded voice or visual introduction. As their instructor you cannot control how students will respond to you but you can make an effort to work with them and get to know them.

Why Online Relationships Matter

The most important reason why relationships matter is that you must work with students to help them succeed. A positive relationship with students helps prevent the online environment from becoming mechanical as it humanizes the learning experience. You become "real" to students and in turn they become "real" to you. At the basis of the word *relationship* is the word *relate* and while it can't be forced, you have an ability to nurture it. For example, you can personalize students' feedback rather than use strictly canned comments. You may never get to know your students but you can still work with them and offer to assist them. Be sure to closely watch your communication and do your best to always assist them. Every class consists of students that rely upon you and this is a reminder that teaching involves much more than classroom management.

Develop Meaningful Relationships

When you ask students to post an introduction at the beginning of the class that represents an ideal ice-breaking activity, one that allows you to guide them with what you want them to share. While fun facts are entertaining, consider the value of what you ask them to post. The goal is to begin to learn something about them that will allow you to understand their developmental needs.

In addition to the introduction you can also offer multiple sources of availability, such as the use of email and instant messaging, as a means of establishing an open dialogue with them. For email, be sure to check it as frequently as you can to reduce students' frustration and anxiety. Instant messaging can be used to hold office hours each week. This creates a perception that you are accessible and approachable, and helps to establish an open connection with them.

All of the interactions that you develop with students can further impact your relationship with them. If you are able to establish rapport with your students, you are more likely to be viewed as approachable. If you are proactive instead of reactive to situations and circumstances, they will discover you possess emotional intelligence. It is up to you as their instructor to make initial and ongoing attempts to develop meaningful relationships. While superficial responses to students' questions and discussion posts is adequate, the ultimate goal is to develop engaging communication so that students will work with you.

Visibility and Credibility

When you develop a strong virtual presence it lets students know you are engaged in the class. It is similar to seeing an instructor present in a traditional classroom; the more the instructor is seen the more comfortable students become. You cannot manage an online class from afar and with your presence you can begin to bridge that distance gap. With the discussion board take time to engage students in a conversation and as they respond be sure to follow-up with them. It is an effective practice to respond to all students at least once for each required discussion question as it shows students you are acknowledging their effort and contributions. It can be challenging with a large class size to post a reply to ever student and if that is the case, try to rotate your responses so that all students eventually receive a reply from you.

Trust is also a significant issue within online classes and something that is challenging to develop in a virtual environment. As students interact with you they begin to assess your credibility. They will likely learn to trust you if they believe what you tell them, and if you are both firm and fair when addressing their issues and requests. Getting to know your students requires effort and time, beyond managing the classroom and completing your required facilitation duties. But the outcome is that the time spent working together is enjoyable for everyone as students feel connected to the class, distance is minimized, and students are fully engaged in the learning process.

Build Relationships with Students that Matter

Developing effective working relationships with students is important for an instructor in any classroom environment; however, relationships developed within an online environment carry a greater significance because the instructor and students have never met. Without a physical presence online instructors must find alternate ways of developing their working relationships with students.

It is possible that this challenge can still exist for an instructor in a traditional classroom, if students only have an opportunity to interact with their instructor during a scheduled class time. However, if an instructor has to rely upon written words alone through classroom posts the relationships with students do not feel as personal as face-to-face interactions. It may only be a perceptual issue for students but it is still important from a relational perspective.

The adult learning process is an active, developmental effort that is dependent upon the student and the instructor being able to work together in a productive manner. While it can exist in a transactional nature it also has a potential to become transformational. The purpose of creating a learning environment that encourages productive interactions is that it can have a positive impact on students' progress and help to improve performance, engagement, and motivation in the class.

A productive working relationship helps the instructor when they need to convey expectations and feedback, it facilitates effective communication, and at the same time it allows students to feel more comfortable expressing their questions and concerns. These positive interactions are also likely to help them feel connected to the class, which in turn can build a sense of community.

Instructors have an ability to develop a personal connection with their students by addressing questions about assignments in a helpful manner, offering constructive feedback about their performance, recognizing their contributions, challenging them to expand their capabilities, discussing resources that are available to meet their developmental needs, and offering strategies that will help them meet their academic goals. When students have developed a strong working relationship with their instructor they are more likely to be engaged in the class, express their ideas, be open to receiving new information, consider how to utilize the feedback provided, and evaluate their existing knowledge and experiences as part of the process of learning. Through these positive relationships, discussions, and interactions with the instructor and others in the class, students are likely to find an environment that is conducive to learning.

Become an Advocate for Your Students

This section will provide you with another perspective about the work of an educator. An educator has many roles to fulfill with every class assigned. They must provide guided instruction and meaningful feedback, manage and control classroom conditions, and facilitate the learning process. The most important aspect of educating students is meeting their developmental needs.

When is an educator most effective with that task? When they develop a mindset that is student centered. That means putting the student first and considering their needs and perspective with every learning activity and interaction. It is an instructional strategy that is both supportive and nurturing, becoming an advocate for every student's success.

A Willingness to Assist

Becoming a student advocate involves demonstrating a caring and compassionate attitude, which requires receiving input from students and replying or responding with a willingness to assist them. This can be accomplished through online class discussions and feedback provided for written assignments. When interacting with students during class discussions it becomes important to read, reflect, and respond with insight to their posts, while building upon what they've written and engaging them in the course materials and topics. For written assignments, it means thoroughly reading and not just glancing at students' papers and instead, highlighting key points and including comments that are meant to further their thinking based upon your knowledge of the subject matter.

Addressing Frustrated Students

It can be challenging at times for an educator to maintain a helpful posture, especially when students feel free post or send messages without considering the tone of their communication and/or demonstrating a lack of respect for the educator's position or authority. However, all concerns, requests, and frustrations hold some degree of validity. There is usually something embedded within this form of aggressive communication that requires consideration. The student may be trying to get attention, even if it is a misguided attempt. Not all students know how to ask for help in a productive manner, which means the educator can use it as a teaching experience.

Use Verbal Communication

Another challenge for educators is providing assistance for students when they do not have the authority to change school policies. For example, there is often a strict late policy in place and it can be difficult to help a student who has fallen behind when they are not allowed to make up the work.

As an advocate it then becomes necessary to guide the students and provide an explanation while demonstrating support as you guide them back on track. Make every response personalized and offer personal contact as you are able to, based upon your schedule. Why is verbal communication more effective? The answer is that email replies can become lengthy and veer off track. A frustrated student can become more aggressive, which means it is better to communicate with a call to provide immediate assistance.

Productive Personal Contact

Personal contact with students can help diffuse disputes, which left unresolved can become a conflict, and allows you to get to the heart of an issue, while building working relationships. It demonstrates that you truly are an advocate for their needs. While communicating with the student through personal contact, ask open-ended questions to engage them in the resolution process. Develop steps for them to take and establish a follow-up contact time-frame. Create an advocacy log and record student names, their issue (in two or three words), and then a follow-up date to check in with them again.

Develop A Physician's Approach

An advocate's approach to addressing students' needs can take a page from the work of a physician. A physician will generally demonstrate a proactive attitude, look beyond symptoms to address potential causes of the underlying issues, and suggest resolution methods that are based upon the needs of the patient. Educators can take the same approach and develop a process of making the rounds or checking in with each student on a regular basis, especially with those students who are losing progress or have been absent from class.

A Proactive Advocate

An advocacy process requires a proactive and responsive approach, instead of reactively addressing issues after they have escalated. This means assessing students individually by examining their classroom performance and academic skill sets, providing a diagnosis based upon root causes instead of symptoms, and providing solutions that support ongoing progress.

An educator can prescribe resources, tools, techniques, and strategies that support success. The goal is to teach, lead, mentor, and guide students as an advocate for their personalized needs. Assist them in the learning process and develop your role as someone who takes a solutions oriented approach. As you become student focused you will find students become responsive and better engaged in the classroom and the learning process.

How to Work with Uncooperative Students

There is an aspect of online teaching that seems inevitable for educators and is likely to occur with every online class. It involves students who either remain distant from you as their instructor or they simply refuse to cooperate with you. Students who have this disposition may make demands about their grades or outcomes, resist viewing and utilizing feedback, or not accept constructive criticism in an objective manner.

Some students may be open to change while others will require time before they will begin to interact directly with you. There will be other students who are going to be challenging simply because they have established patterns of thought or negative beliefs about instructors in general. A perfect class would be easy to teach as every student would be responsive to your communication. But that isn't always the case and it will help your work as an educator to have strategies that can be used as part of your teaching style or practice.

Maintaining Communication Attempts

Have you ever talked to a student and you knew from the moment the conversation began that nothing you could say would change their attitude or disposition? They have already established a closed mindset and it could be based upon perceptions or experience they've had with other instructors or the school. Working with online students poses a unique challenge. You can be open to working with them and request a conversation by phone only to discover that students simply do not respond to you. I know from my experience as an educator that students are either not conditioned to personalized interaction or they want to retain their anonymity. Trying to break through that type of mindset barrier can be challenging, even with the best of intentions.

My philosophy as an online educator is to respond to student emails within two hours on weekdays. On the weekend I will watch for emails and answer anything with pressing issues or concerns. While that establishes a level of responsiveness on my part, students may still not respond to those attempts. I know from my work as a faculty peer reviewer that it is not uncommon to find instructors who wait much longer to respond to questions.

You should develop your own regular schedule. Where an uncooperative attitude comes into play is when you want to talk with students about their progress and they simply ignore your attempt or worse, they respond in a hostile manner or the tone of their communication is aggressive. When students hold onto a disposition like that it can be difficult to obtain their cooperation so they can communicate in a meaningful manner.

A Student's Perspective

When students are non-responsive, or they do respond and seem to be uncooperative, it is often done so from a reactive state of mind. From my experience working with online students, there have been times when a student has viewed their cumulative grade or feedback for an assignment and had a reactive response. They may have believed that the grade was unjust, they "worked hard" on the assignment and deserved a perfect score, or there can be any other number of reasons. Those students will either remain silent, finally reach out when their frustration has built up, or eventually disengage from the class.

Those reactions may be tied to beliefs that were built upon unrealistic expectations. For example, a student may believe that any amount of effort exerted on their part should equate to a certain grade. It is certainly understandable that students may have a reaction and possibly with strong emotions; however, it is not acceptable to respond back with an aggressive demeanor. It serves no purpose and works against the development of a productive working relationship as they will resist any further attempts to provide helpful feedback and constructive criticism.

Forms of Uncooperative Students

There are different types of uncooperative students. There is the shy student who may feel intimidated by their instructor, there may be a type a student who feels fully in charge of their education and doesn't prefer any other interactions with their instructor, and then there are students who believe they know what is best for their development and won't communicate unless their instructor is able to persuade them to change their perspective.

There are other forms of uncooperative students and due to the nature of an online class you may not get to know what their mindset is until you communicate with them.

Consider this example: You have an uncooperative student who contacts you but they will not listen to you. You can either try to find common ground and discuss their progress or request another time to talk so that they can regain their emotional balance.

While it is not pleasant working with students who are not responsive or uncooperative, or they are difficult to communicate with, it can help you learn more about yourself as an educator and prompt a time of professional self-evaluation. This is a time to ask yourself what can be learned so you are able to either reaffirm your teaching method is on target or make self-corrections as needed.

Steps to Working with Uncooperative Students

There are strategies that I have used and taught online faculty to use, which you may also find helpful as well.

#1. Be Proactive

The first step an online instructor can take is to be proactive in their approach to working with students. Encourage open communication through scheduled office hours, with availability for one-on-one telephone appointments, and include notations in your feedback that encourages students to ask questions.

#2. Make Outreach Attempts

A challenge for online teaching is the possibility that students may slowly disengage from their class. When students are not communicative it can either mean they are not cooperating or they are in the process of withdrawing from the class. You may not know the reason why until you talk to the students so make every effort to reach them.

#3. Keep the Momentum Going

Once you are able to gain cooperation with your students, and you have established a productive working relationship them, don't assume that it is set and complete for the duration of your class. Maintain your efforts to keep them engaged and continue to offer personalized assistance throughout the duration of the class.

#4. Addressing an Uncooperative Mindset

When a student does not contact you and they have an uncooperative mindset it means there is an underlying need or negative perspective that may or may not be easily changed. In your outreach attempts you can offer to discuss the specifics about their progress in class and then decide upon an action plan. If you are able to speak with the student by phone and they become aggressive or threatening, it may be time to discontinue the call and talk with them during a less emotional time.

#5. Teach with Compassion

The best advice for working with any student, cooperative or uncooperative, is to always have their best interests in mind as your work with them and address their academic needs. It may be challenging at times, especially if they are utilizing inappropriate communication. You may not always handle every situation perfectly because you can still experience natural human emotions; however, teach with a caring mindset and students will likely respond in a favorable manner.

Maintaining Open Communication

For online classes, communication in the form of online posts and emails may feel impersonal. This can be overcome by being highly self-conscious of the tone used and how it may be interpreted. As to working with online students, make it your goal to always maintain open communication.

What does this mean? It is a mindset of welcoming your students' attempts to communicate directly with you, whether by email, phone, or other methods that you have established for them to use. When they send you an email, demonstrate through your reply that you are glad they have reached out to you and do your best to welcome future communication.

As an educator, be the one who demonstrates a cooperative demeanor as a means of modeling it for your students. For those students who resist your attempts, or they simply won't respond to you, they might not ever change their approach. Be sure to make outreach attempts that demonstrate consistency and a caring attitude at all times. Make it your goal to do what you can to be open and responsive to all students - even those who challenge you. Being an effective educator is an ongoing learning process of learning through trial and practice, and even error at times, how to gain cooperation and responsiveness from your students.

Why Online Students Fail Their Classes

Failing a class never feels good for a student. In a traditional classroom students have an opportunity to discuss their progress and obtain immediate feedback from their instructor. While they may or may not choose to try to work with their instructor, they know that on the scheduled class days an instructor is present and available. If a student isn't present in class an instructor will notice that absence immediately.

On the other hand, failing an online class is usually associated with feelings of discouragement, hopelessness, and a lack of care or concern from the instructor. Student disengagement from an online class usually occurs over time, as a culmination of failed attempts, an inability to make a meaningful connection to the class, and a lack of a productive working relationship with the instructor.

If an instructor does not maintain an active presence and is not responsive to the needs of their students, those students who are gradually disengaging may not be noticed until it is too late to connect them back to the class.

The nature of distance learning presents inherent challenges for students and their instructors. There are reasons why students fail their classes and knowing the possible reasons why allows instructors to help prevent it from occurring through the use of proactive instructional strategies.

When Students Start an Online Class

Starting a new online class can be challenging, especially for the first class that students are required to take. They are expected to start their classes and be able to quickly function in this virtual environment and in a highly productive manner. There are academic skills that must be learned, related to writing and communicating in virtual class, and supportive habits that need to be quickly developed. This includes learning how to manage their time well so that they do not become overwhelmed. There is also the reality of working in a technologically-enabled class and whether or not it aligns with their initial perception of what is required as an online student.

Students typically begin their classes with a hopeful mindset as their degree is often linked to career goals or future plans, even if they do not know exactly what to expect as a student. This means that students generally do not begin with a sense of failure in mind, although some may not be certain that they can meet the demands and express their uncertainty. Over time, and as setbacks and challenges are experienced, the word failure may become part of their mindset. This is problematic as it can interrupt the best efforts and intentions of students, unless an instructor can intervene.

Instructors know when their students have gotten off track, especially if they are actively involved in the class, and they can intervene through contact attempts or coaching efforts. There is a stigma associated with failing a class, as it is assumed someone contributed to it or there were other factors that caused the students to fail - such as actions or a lack of action on the part of the instructor.

Instructors hold an expectation that students must meet the required academic standards; however, students may not be prepared to meet those standards or have a mindset that is not receptive to change. Overall, student success depends upon a collaborative effort initiated by the instructor and accepted by the students.

The Nature of Students and Failing

When students began an online program they rarely receive an academic skills pre-assessment as a condition of enrollment with many of the for-profit online schools and that means their first class sets the stage for what they are going to experience. Students who have unrealistic expectations about this type of learning environment may find that it can cause a barrier to their developmental progress if those perceptions are not correct, and changing those beliefs takes time and practice, along with support of an instructor.

Another factor that contributes to a decline in student performance is their approach to completing the required learning activities. If students have established patterns of performance that are not productive it may undermine their ability to succeed or make progress. Instructors know when students are not performing to the best of their capabilities and it is reflected in a declining GPA. When students see their grades decline they may not know what to do at first, especially if their perceived locus of control is outside of their ability to change conditions. The challenge for instructors is a matter of working with students who may or may not be receptive to their offer of assistance.

Academic Preparedness

For the field of distance learning the phrase non-traditional student has become common as a means of describing the unique needs of students who enroll in online classes. Many non-traditional students are academically under-prepared, which means that they start their classes not being fully prepared or possessing all of the required academic skills.

There is a learning curve for new students and their level of academic preparedness makes a significant difference with how quickly they can adapt. They must learn to be prepared for the class requirements and develop a time management plan. However, not every student knows what skills are needed and it may take time to learn what is expected of them. Becoming academically prepared takes time and practice, and it also requires resources that the school and instructors need to provide them.

Accountability: Student or Teacher?

Accountability involves holding someone responsible, often to a predetermined standard. Cumulative grades or a GPA and passing a class are typical standards used to measure progress throughout a degree program. Instructors must hold students accountable and that requires looking beyond classroom management duties and being aware of how students are progressing. This becomes a challenge for instructors as they know that students who resist becoming accountable, or perceive that any guidance provided suggesting a need for improvement is picking on them or being harsh, will likely provide negative comments on an end-of-course survey.

Students need to be responsive to their instructors' feedback and outreach attempts throughout the class as that can help keep them on track. As an example, waiting until the last week of class to get caught up is not an effective strategy for students to follow. Not only has there been a missed learning opportunity, when assignments or activities have not been completed, online instructors generally have minimal flexibility with regards to changing the established late policy or assignment deadlines. Instructors are held to a high standard of accountability and in turn they are also expected to hold students accountable for their compliance with the established policies and procedures.

Success Strategies

To help students succeed instructors need to monitor their progress and pay attention to their involvement in class. There will be warning signs along the way, such as a poorly written paper or under-developed discussion post. Instructors have to decide what action to take as outreach is a crucial component of reducing the risk for failure. Students can either accept an offer for assistance and the need to be involved in the process of self-development or they can continue to believe that they have no control over their progress, which can stall their growth. In order to be successful and reduce the possibility of failing a class, instructors can teach students to use the following strategies:

Self-Assessment:

Conduct a periodic self-assessment of their skills and progress. This can be a matter of encouraging self-reflection through feedback provided and/or offering tools and resources for skills assessment. The purpose is to help students to focus on their strengths first and use those strengths to address areas of needed development.

Use the Power of Beliefs:

Examine their belief system and what they believe they can accomplish. Henry Ford stated: "Whether you think you can, or you think you can't, either way you are right". That best summarizes the power of a student's mindset and their ability to believe in being successful whenever they make an attempt - when they participate in a discussion or submit a written assignment. A positive belief in what they are capable of accomplishing will support their efforts and encourage their continued progress.

Develop a Support System:

Teach students how to develop a support system and utilize it for encouragement and help. For some students in an online class the only immediate support available may be other students and that is why it is important to help students feel that they are part of a learning community. An instructor can also serve as part of that support system, if there is an interest in being involved in each student's developmental progress.

Develop Communication:

Teach students to communicate with their instructor about challenges and areas where they are struggling - and be willing to accept feedback received. This is not an easy goal to meet and it is one that requires the development of a productive working relationship between the instructor and their students. More importantly, there has to be a level of trust between them and a willingness for both to listen to each other. In distance learning that may seem too challenging to attempt; however, those instructors who truly care about their students will find a way to bridge that distance gap.

The Power of Retention

When students are assigned to an online class they are under the direction and care of their instructors, and they should be able to expect to receive guidance and support. Instructors can help students learn to develop their academic skills, find needed resources, and maintain momentum throughout the class. Instructors also need to conduct outreach attempts in a genuine and caring manner.

The impact of failing a class is experienced by both the instructor and the student. For the instructor, it can influence their standing in the school and for the student, it may have a negative impact on their overall degree progress. Failure can be avoided if instructors are willing to take the time necessary to monitor and coach their students, and students do their part by accepting accountability for their involvement in the learning process and develop a positive belief about their capacity to learn.

---

6 Strategies to Help Students Overcome the Risk of Failure

The retention rate for many online schools is lower than traditional schools and there are many reasons why students fail to complete or discontinue their degree program. The factors may vary, including the cost per credit hour, school policies, and the quality of the courses offered. Instructors have little control over many of those factors but what they can help with is the classroom environment that they are responsible for maintaining.

With every class, students are at risk for failure because of the nature of a virtual environment and interactions with others. New students have the greatest risk and the most challenging learning curve. When students take their first class it is a time when their perceptions and expectations meet the reality of working in an online class. Every subsequent class requires adapting in some manner, to a new instructor and set of requirements. This creates a risk or possibility for students to fail.

All instructors, not just those who teach entry point classes, are responsible for nurturing the development of their students.

This means that teaching is not just a function with a checklist of duties, it is a process that requires full engagement and support for the progress of every student. With online classes it is possible for students to gradually disengage, if they become frustrated or their motivation wanes.

If an instructor doesn't notice a student's struggle or does but fails to conduct some form of outreach, that student may disengage completely within a short period of time. There are proactive strategies an instructor can implement as part of their instructional strategy, to maintain awareness of class conditions and lessen the likelihood of students failing to complete the course.

Student Perceptions of Failure

Students start their classes with a variety of feelings. There is a sense of a fresh start, mixed with the possibility of uncertainty, apprehension, and/or anxiety - especially if they do not know their new instructor.

The first week requires students to "hit the ground running" so to speak, and few begin by thinking they will fail unless they have determined they do not have the required academic skills and cannot develop those skills quickly enough.

Students think about failure most when they put in what they believe to be their best effort and receive feedback that conflicts with that belief and/or they watch their cumulative grade as an indicator of their progress and it continues to decline no matter how hard they try. Some students are not bothered by less than perfect outcomes and others will believe they have failed if they did not earn all "A" grades.

There is a perception that grades are somehow tied to a student's self-worth and that causes those students to give up easily when they perceive they have failed.

The Challenge of Academic Under-Preparedness

Many online schools have minimal entrance requirements for accepting new students, especially related to existing academic skills. Instructors in undergraduate entry point classes know this condition more than anyone else. It is possible to have students who are so academically under-prepared that the focus of the entire class is on learning basic literacy skills.

The ability of students to progress is directly related to their receptiveness to feedback, ability to cooperate, persistence in the midst of challenges, and the nature of the instructor. If an instructor demands compliance, rather than support and encourage development, it will create a barrier to progress that can set the stage for failure. The very first class, even the first few classes, determines whether students will become equipped to meet the academic rigors of their degree program. The support that the school and instructors offer is critical to helping prepare students for success.

What it Means to Be Accountable

Students are expected to follow the required policies and procedures, complete the required learning activities, perform to the best of their abilities, remain highly motivated, and be actively engaged in the learning process as a standard ideal. What instructors use as a guide for assessing the progress made by students for meeting those expectations is what they can "see" in the classroom and that consists of class and discussion posts, along with the effort and attempt made with the learning activities. In order to hold students accountable for meeting these expectations, instructors must make them clear at the start of a class and encourage students to ask questions.

It is possible that expectations can vary from one instructor to another, which means instructors need to clearly communicate what they will hold students accountable for and provide both clarification and reminders on a regular basis. What may seem clear from an instructor's perspective may not be interpreted that way the first time a student reads it, especially during the first week of class when they are trying to read and process all of the new materials and information. One method I've used is to create a section in the course syllabus that outlines my expectations and then I will refer back to it on occasion, as a reminder for the students.

Strategies to Reduce the Risk of Failure

To help your students learn to meet the required expectations, and prepare them for success in their class, there are six strategies any instructor can include as part of their online teaching strategy, regardless of the subject being taught.

#1. Establish Clearly Defined Expectations:

If you expect students to follow your particular requirements, they need to clearly understand what you expect. You can add a section to the course syllabus that outlines your expectations, whether it is a specific number of days you expect them to participate or the use of sources to support the development of their posts and papers. When you post weekly messages, be sure to include reminders about these expectations when needed. One method I have used to reinforce the expectations for written assignments is to develop a rubric and provide it at the start of the class week.

#2. Work to Develop Open Communication:

Working in a virtual classroom environment can be intimidating for some students, especially if they feel isolated from their instructor, so it is imperative that productive working relationships are established. This will encourage students to reach out and ask for help whenever they have a question or need assistance.

Be certain to have a supportive and helpful attitude as the first time a student asks for assistance will determine if they are encouraged or discouraged from asking for help again. The tone used in all responses will be interpreted so I often read my posts and messages aloud to ensure they are as effective as they can be.

#3. Teach Students the Power of Self-Assessment:

Instructors can help students learn to monitor their own progress, the skills and knowledge they have acquired, and the beliefs they hold about their ability to succeed. To monitor their progress, I will teach students to use some of the formative assessment techniques, such as a one-minute paper.

To help students with the knowledge acquisition process I will teach them to use note-taking methods that they can then utilize later as a self-quiz. As to the development of skills, I make sure to note their accomplishments and progress in the feedback provided. Finally, I will talk about self-beliefs in messages I post and conversations I have with students - either by phone or through other one-on-one communication.

#4. Provide Feedback and Follow-Through:

Providing a completed rubric or letter grade is never enough when it comes to supporting students and addressing their developmental needs. I provide interactive feedback that addresses both the content and the mechanics of what was written. I add in comments via track changes in a Word document or wording typed directly into the paper, and I share my expertise, experience, and additional thoughts.

I also ask questions in my feedback as a means of engaging the students further and then I encourage them to ask questions. The purpose is to create interactive feedback that prompts follow-up with them. The follow-through is necessary whenever I have a student who is struggling, not making progress, making the same mistakes, or facing any other challenges. I want to make certain they have read the feedback and provide them with an opportunity to discuss their progress.

#5. Be a Teacher, Facilitator, Mentor, and Coach:

Every instructor can lead the way for their students and be a guide that helps to support them in a servant leadership role. While many online schools like to call an instructor a facilitator, the many responsibilities that an instructor has involves much more than facilitating a process.

Instructors need to be aware of how their students are performing and help them find resources when needed, teach them productive habits when it seems they cannot accomplish the required tasks each week, and offer support when they question their ability to do well or have self-doubts. All of these roles help to teach students to persist and it encourages a growth mindset.

#6. Conduct Outreach on an Ongoing Basis:

While this will require extra time on the part of the instructor, it can certainly make a difference in the long term success of the students. Instructors must be aware of the class conditions and alert for students who are struggling and disengaging from the class so that they can be proactive in outreach attempts before it becomes a chronic problem that results in complete withdrawal from the class.

I've found that an extra email or phone call goes a long way towards establishing a bond with my students and helps to bridge the distance gap with them. Most of the time one outreach contact in some form is enough to re-engage the students; however, there are some students who feel hopeless and believe that circumstances happen to them rather than having control over their own outcomes.

Those students require much more patience and personalized attention, which some instructors do not like to do, but in the end I've found it is worth my time as it helps to address the needs of my students.

Failure is Inevitable

It is highly unlikely that every class will have a 100% retention rate, especially for online schools that have open admissions policies. However, through my work with online faculty development, and experience with online teaching, I have found that there is a direct correlation between the retention rate of a class and both the level and quality of the instructor's involvement. Clearly there are students who are not well-suited to the online classroom environment and this includes those students who are inflexible, uncooperative, and unwilling to adapt.

But there are many students who are able to work successfully in a virtual class and if they experience challenges or frustrations the instructor's presence and assistance can prevent disengagement. Students respond well to an instructor who makes the extra effort to guide their development and they become more receptive to coaching and feedback. If an instructor cares about how they teach, as much as what they teach, it is possible to reduce the risk of students failing.

Why Students Need to Trust Their Instructors

As an instructor, do you ever consider the element of trust and its relevance to your classroom facilitation? Is it important or necessary for students to trust their instructor in order for the process of learning to occur? Students are often assigned to a class without knowing who their instructor will be until the first day. They may believe or trust that their needs will be met or they might take a wait and see approach.

Until students get to know their instructor better it is possible that they will allow their perceptions and prior experiences to dictate how receptive they are to the development of working relationships and what they begin to believe about the instructor's ability to facilitate the class. When an instructor is able to connect with their students and build productive relationships they are also likely to develop trust, which in turn can have a positive impact on the learning environment.

When students trust their instructor, they develop a reliance upon them in several ways. For example, they trust the instructor will help them meet their developmental needs, they rely upon the instructor's experience with the process of learning, and they have an expectation that the instructor will know how to bring the course materials to life in a way that facilitates the acquisition of knowledge.

The element of trust is also an essential component of working relationships as students will only be receptive to someone they believe they can trust. While an instructor can demand compliance with policies and procedures, they cannot demand that a student will devote the level of involvement they expect is necessary. If the student trusts their instructor, they are likely to follow his or her lead and become a willing participant in the learning process.

Students do not develop trust for their instructor automatically; rather it occurs through a process of ongoing interactions. Often the instructor's approach determines the outcome of these interactions and this includes the tone of their communication, their attitude that is perceptually interpreted, and their responsiveness to students' questions and concerns. Gaining trust requires time and skillful effort on the part of the instructor and it is easily negated through periods of conflict or miscommunication.

When trust is successfully established, instructors often find that students become receptive to their feedback, coaching, and constructive criticism. This occurs when students believe that their instructor wants them to succeed and maintains their best interest as a priority. As a result, students are more likely to review the feedback provided, implement suggestions and utilize resources, and be engaged in the class.

Instructors may not be able to control the formation of trust; however, they can influence its development by considering how they interact with students and the importance of building meaningful connections.

End of Course Evaluations

You've just been notified that an end of course student evaluation summary has been completed and is available for your review.

Do you take time to look at the report and consider what students have written?

Often newer instructors will take the time to review the reports to help guide development of their facilitation skills; whereas, more experienced instructors may feel comfortable enough with their facilitation practice that they do not believe there is a need to examine the reports.

Regardless of your present skill set level or length of experience as an instructor the end of course evaluation offers information that can inform your instructional strategies and have an impact on your approach to classroom teaching.

The Students' Perspective

When students are provided with an end of course evaluation they may perceive this as an opportunity to voice their opinions or comments about the course and the instructor, or they may be afraid to complete the form believing that the instructor will see the results prior to final grades being submitted.

What is common for student responses is that they will be motivated to complete the evaluation because of a very positive experience in the classroom or a negative experience with the school, classroom, or their instructor, especially if they have no other avenue to express their thoughts and feelings.

Critical Self Reflection

An effective method for reviewing student evaluations is to include it as part of your critical self-reflection about your classroom facilitation practice. It is helpful to reflect upon your class and its overall performance on a periodic basis so you can determine what is working well and what isn't. If you have developed a strong sense of your strengths and facilitation skills you will be able to quickly ascertain if the results of these evaluations are an accurate reflection of the students' experience in the classroom, as well as their interactions with you.

What may offer you the most insight about your class and the students' perspective of the class are the comments that students provide for open-ended questions. For students that are not satisfied for some reason these written comments may indicate why their expectations were not met.

Your Mindset Matters

As you review the evaluations it may be easy to focus on a negative comment rather than consider the overall results, especially if your school has strict standards or teaching measures that you are expected to uphold in order to maintain your status as an instructor. If you believe that any of these reports will have a negative impact on your standing with school, it is important to talk to your department chair or the person in charge of monitoring your progress. All of the results can inform your teaching practice, including those that may not appear to be positive in nature.

For students that had a meaningful classroom experience this likely indicates what strategies are working well overall. For students that had a negative experience you may learn about certain aspects of the class, assignment instructions, course materials, or any other element of the class that could benefit from additional clarification or follow-up.

An end of course evaluation is a tool utilized by most schools as a means of gauging such aspects as quality of learning, students' expectations, and instructor effectiveness. An effective approach is to not live in fear of these evaluations and instead maintain open communication with your students throughout the class so that there are no surprises when these reports are received. It may be helpful to check in with your students on occasion to discuss their progress and address any questions or concerns at that time.

Take time to review the end of course evaluations and allow it to provide you with a self-development opportunity, one that can have a positive impact on your classroom teaching. You may discover aspects of your instructional practice that are working well and should be continued, while there are areas of your instruction that can be improved upon, changed, or replaced.

End of Chapter Check-In

What Have You Learned?

What Are Your Strengths?

What Are Your Developmental Areas?

What Will You Apply to Your Teaching Practice?

CHAPTER 3.
THE IMPACT OF STUDENT BELIEFS

Student Beliefs and Learning

When a student begins a class, a factor that can have a direct impact on their level of involvement in that class is their beliefs. This is an aspect of online teaching that may be far removed from immediate consideration, especially if the length of the class is short and the instructor is devoting all of their time to classroom management. However, facilitation of the adult learning process may become more effective if the power and effect of these beliefs is better understood.

Student Beliefs

The beliefs that students hold include what they accept as a perceived truth about their ability and potential to learn. These beliefs may be subconsciously held or consciously recognized, formed through a process of ongoing interactions and prior experiences. Students often seek confirmation of these beliefs, instead of questioning why they believe what they do, which in turn may determine the actions taken in the classroom, including the time, energy, and effort they devote to the process of learning.

The beliefs that students hold about their academic abilities and capability to participate in the learning process will also influence their persistence when faced with challenges and is a determining factor for their grades and course outcomes. Their beliefs also shape their attitude about learning, the interactions they have with other students, and their working relationships with instructors. When beliefs are subconsciously held they eventually become recognized through interactions within the classroom environment, especially during discussions when those beliefs are challenged or questioned.

An Instructor's Role

How can an instructor directly influence, guide, and help shape students' beliefs, especially if those students do not have a positive attitude about their capabilities? This can be accomplished by helping them discover that they have a greater capacity to learn. An instructor who effectively guides students may shape their beliefs by engaging them in the process of learning, encouraging their efforts and attempts to participate, and finding resources that help to meet their developmental needs.

In contrast, an instructor is likely to find that simply telling students they must become an active participant is less effective than guiding them through the process. Students are self-directed by nature and they often come to the classroom with specific needs, which are influenced by their beliefs about what they are capable of doing.

Changing a belief system, especially one that has been held for a long period of time, may not happen overnight or within a short period of time. It is the accumulation of positive experiences and meaningful interactions that can change their beliefs in the long run. An instructor who encourages self-discovery and reminds students they have a greater capacity to learn will likely find this approach is much more effective in shaping their beliefs than demanding participation in the learning process.

Students are more likely to be engaged in the class if they believe they can learn and it will meet their learning needs. This is an example of the power that beliefs can hold for the process of adult learning and how an instructor can influence those beliefs.

What Do You Believe about Your Students?

Before an instructor attempts to understand what their students believe, they should examine their own belief systems. Here are some questions to consider: Have you considered what assumptions you hold about your students at the start of class? Do you assume that students are prepared to participate in the learning process and motivated to complete their assignments, or do they need your guidance to get started? What do you believe about your students in general and do those beliefs change as the class progresses? Finally, do you believe that providing additional assistance is handholding or necessary to support your students' progress?

An Instructor's Beliefs

An instructor's initial beliefs may include perceptions, whether valid or not, about their students' abilities, which can include their need for support, feedback, expression, and ongoing meaningful interactions. When you consider factors that are important for the learning process, from the perspective of your students, you might list factors such as academic skills, self-motivation, and time management. However, what any student needs to succeed over the long term is perseverance, persistence, and a growth mindset.

What instructors believe about their students may inform or influence their approach to teaching and these perceptions are likely to change through interactions and discussions. For example, negative interactions can affect the disposition of an instructor and how they approach working with their students. A helpful approach for effective classroom teaching involves conducting a self-examination of the beliefs held and the impact of those beliefs on the process of teaching and learning. Those beliefs are also reflected in the tone and general disposition of instructors when they are working with students.

Conducting a Belief Self-Check

Examine the beliefs you hold about your students by looking at the words you use to describe your students. Would your description include the words potential, capable, flawed, or self-motivated? Next, consider what you believe your students' needs are at the beginning of your class. Would their needs include guidance, support, or personal and professional development?

Finally, take into consideration what your role is as an instructor, along what your involvement in the class should be, and how you will interact with your students. Will a description of your tasks, duties, and responsibilities include mentor, coach, teacher, or facilitator? Do you believe that you need to facilitate a process, teach your students about something specific, or tell them what it is they need to learn?

These beliefs create a lens through which you view your students and it is important to reevaluate what you believe on a regular basis so that you can determine if they are accurate and supportive of their growth and development. This will also help to create a shift in your perspective of online teaching overall.

Beliefs: Validity & Impact

Once you have examined your beliefs you can then consider what factors have influenced and shaped what you now believe about your students and their potential. It is likely that the culmination of interactions, experiences, assignments, responsiveness (or lack thereof to feedback), along with discussion responses from prior classes, have had a direct bearing on your current perception. What you believe will translate into how you interact with your students. As part of this self-examination you have an opportunity now to evaluate the validity of your beliefs and determine the impact of your current perspective about the classroom environment.

Beliefs can be limiting when students are viewed collectively as a class that is succeeding or failing, willing or resistant, capable or limited in their abilities. One method of beginning to overcome the development of a single perspective about your class is to ask students to post an introduction at the beginning of the class so you can shift your view from seeing students as a group to evaluating students on an individual basis.

Your perspective will be further updated as you begin evaluating students' performance. What can be helpful is to try to weigh their work and evaluate their participation individually and keep in mind that every student has a capacity to learn and change, if they are provided with the necessary instructional support, tools, and resources.

A Need for Positive Beliefs

Development of a nurturing classroom environment that supports students' learning requires instructors to have positive beliefs about their abilities. As your class progresses ask yourself if can you develop a positive view of your students and maintain that belief despite their initial setbacks, questions, frustrations, and developmental challenges. You can either have a restricted view of your students, based upon generalizations, or you can have a broader view of students that sees their individual potential.

Help Students Nurture Positive Beliefs

Teaching students will become much more effective if beliefs are examined and understood, both the beliefs of the instructor and their students. While this requires a level of involvement with students that may be difficult to develop with the time provided for a class, instructors can always monitor their own beliefs and support students as they make progress during the class. Being aware of what students believe will help instructors better understand how to approach someone who is struggling in any aspect of the class or with their performance and needs to develop supportive beliefs.

Influence What Your Students Believe

At its very essence, beliefs that students hold are pre-conceived ideas, whether it is about learning, the classroom environment, their involvement and participation, or their instructors. A common example is that a student may believe their best effort is enough or is satisfactory for acceptable classroom performance. Another common belief is that trying hard should result in the best grade or outcome possible.

Some students state that "all instructors" are unfair and have this belief because their expectations weren't met or they didn't receive an expected grade or outcome. An instructor can recognize beliefs like this if a student states they didn't deserve a grade received, which is often a reflection of their locus of control. They will either view their grades and outcomes as something that happens to them or something they are in direct control of regardless of the grade received. The following instructional strategies can help instructors influence student beliefs.

#1. Influence Student Behaviors

Regardless of how long a class lasts, even if it is an entire semester in length, it may be challenging for instructors to learn about the beliefs of every student or tailor their instruction to each individual student. What an instructor can do is to establish clear expectations, provide support and feedback, and influence beliefs by understanding what behavioral aspects of a student's performance need to change because at the heart of a student's performance are behaviors.

Students need to develop self-efficacy or a belief in their ability to complete their tasks, along with self-regulation or an ability to control their behaviors and manage their emotions. They must learn to persist when they are challenged to learn new behaviors, especially as related to how they perform, and they need supportive work habits to maximize their productivity. If an instructor can teach students to persist and discover their internal self-motivation, it will help them develop new habitual behaviors that support positive beliefs about their capabilities.

#2. Help Students Discover Their Capacity

Once you understand what you and your students believe, you can then work to influence those beliefs. The question to consider is this: can an instructor directly influence, guide, and help shape a student's beliefs if they do not have a positive attitude about their capabilities?

This can be best accomplished by helping the student discover that they have a capacity to learn, regardless of how well or poorly they have performed to date, and it is possible to improve with time and practice.

An instructor who effectively guides the student may shape their beliefs by engaging them in the process of learning, encouraging their efforts and attempts to participate, and finding resources that help to meet their developmental needs.

In contrast, an instructor is likely to find that simply telling students they must become an active participant is less effective than one that involves guiding them through the process. Student are self-directed by nature and they often have specific needs, which are influenced by their beliefs about what they are capable of doing.

#3. Use the Power of Persuasion

Students, especially new students, may need to alter or completely discard beliefs that are not serving them well and develop new beliefs. However, changing a belief, especially one that has been held for a long period of time, may not happen overnight or within the short period of time allowed during a class. It is the accumulation of positive experiences and meaningful interactions that can change a student's beliefs in the long run, along with the development of habitual behaviors to support it.

An instructor who encourages self-discovery and prompts students to reassess their beliefs about being involved in the learning process is much more effective in shaping their beliefs than demanding that they change and accept (without question) that their beliefs are inaccurate or not valid. Students are unlikely to change unless they see a specific reason and this can be recognized through persuasive feedback and conversations that are supportive and nurtures their growth mindset.

Beliefs Manifest into Actions

Every student begins a class with an existing belief system, whether or not they recognize the basis of what they believe about learning and their role in the process. Their beliefs are manifested in the actions they take, the effort they make, and the attitudes they hold. However, those beliefs are tested through their involvement in the class, when their expectations meet the reality of being a student and the outcomes of their efforts are received in the form of a grade.

If students have a positive belief system and work in a nurturing environment, they are likely to persist even when challenged. It is up to the instructor to encourage students, create conditions that support their efforts, and develop nurturing relationships. A student is most successful when they sustain beliefs that are self-empowering and instructors can promote this by also believing in the best of them.

End of Chapter Check-In

What Have You Learned?

What Are Your Strengths?

What Are Your Developmental Areas?

What Will You Apply to Your Teaching Practice?

CHAPTER 4.
LEARNING IN A VIRTUAL ENVIRONMENT

What Makes an Online Class "Real" to Students?

The for-profit online school industry has received a great deal of attention over the past few years and the reasons have involved recruiting practices, low retention rates, and the failure to pay student loan rates. Recently there was an article about one online school that was being audited, specifically regarding the level of faculty to student interactions.

This particular school offers competency-based online degree programs and students are completing their degrees without being enrolled in traditional online classes. The underlying reason for the audit is related to the programs being qualified to receive federal aid. In order for students to be eligible to receive federal aid there must be "significant instructor to student interactions" and if those interactions aren't present the programs become ineligible for aid.

The online university in question doesn't offer traditional class terms and instead students work at their own pace and take pre-developed assessments to demonstrate that they possess the required knowledge and competencies. Whenever a student needs assistance, instructors are available during set hours and there is an option to schedule an appointment with an instructor for one-on-one instruction.

The audit seeks to determine if those are enough interactions to categorize it as an online learning program or a set of correspondence courses. The findings of this audit could have a significant impact on the implementation of competency-based programs, which many online schools have considered implementing or are in the process of adding to their programs.

From my perspective as an online educator this audit brings to light an important aspect of online learning that goes beyond the question of the number of interactions, and it is the role of the instructor in the learning process. I understand the purpose of competency-based programs is to acknowledge the past experience of students and allow them to work at their own pace. However, what happens to the role of the instructor who is no longer actively involved in online classes? Are instructors still teaching students if their primary responsibilities involve scheduling appointments with students, evaluating assessments, and answering questions?

This leads to another question that is relevant for all distance learning programs: what makes online learning "real" for students?

Correspondence, Self-Paced Courses

At its very essence a correspondence course is self-paced in nature, with or without specific completion deadlines. Originally this concept began as a mail-in course with required reading materials provided and a test or assignment was to be completed and mailed in. These courses were eventually replaced almost completely by online courses.

It is still possible for an online course to be established as a correspondence course, especially if there is little or no instructor involvement in the class and it is designed to be self-paced in nature. This approach is often utilized in continuing education programs that do not offer degree programs and credit hours.

Some program directors believe that an online course is adequately structured if an instructor is available to answer questions when needed or they are present during a specified time throughout the duration of the course.

But consider what that same approach would be like in a traditional college. Students would be required to sit in a class and study, the instructor visits the class once or twice a semester, and/or the instructor has office hours on campus if a student wants to schedule an appointment. Is that the best way for adults to learn? They can certainly learn on their own but then why go to a class at all? More importantly, what does their degree really mean by the time they have completed it?

How Learning Becomes Transformational

At the heart of higher education is a belief that learning should be transformative in nature and that is the missing component with self-paced online courses. For example, with graduate level self-paced courses some educators believe that these students don't need interactions with instructors, that their skills are advanced because of the degrees they have already completed. They may also believe written assignments aren't necessary and a quiz will suffice. The same is true for discussions, that instructor involvement isn't always necessary or adequate participation could be provided by the instructor through a pre-developed posts.

From my perspective, that isn't meaningful online learning and it isn't transformative. Students need the instructor's involvement and more importantly, they need the instructor's active presence to bring the course and course materials to life. Interactions can be transformative, not only with questions that must be answered but class discussions and feedback as well.

What does an online class become when students have questions but immediate contact with an instructor is not an option? Or class discussions occur without an instructor present to prompt engagement and ongoing conversations? Can students learn if their only involvement with an instructor occurs through feedback provided for a written assignment?

Higher education is meant to transform students, through the development of academic skills and the acquisition of knowledge. More importantly, higher education has the potential to transform the way that students think - and that is how students learn.

What Makes Online Classes "Real" to Students

From my experience, online classes become "real" to students when they feel a personal connection in some manner. It begins with a sense of belonging and community as they interact with other students and continues as they work one-on-one with their instructors.

This is not an automatic process and it doesn't occur quickly. If students perceive their instructor isn't actively involved, doesn't seem concerned with their academic well-being, or isn't responsive to their questions and concerns, they can slowly begin to disengage from the class.

Another manner in which the online class becomes "real" occurs when students participate in class discussions and gain new insights and perspectives about the course topics. When they read the course materials they may or may not connect with that information and it is dependent upon whether or not they are able to comprehend it, relate to it, and connect its meaning to the real world. An instructor helps students develop this connection to the class and the course subject matter.

Competency-Based Programs and Higher Education

What does this mean for competency-based programs?

The trend to change the traditional model of learning and move towards this approach continues to grow. The outcome of the audit may or may not change the view of program directors and educators once the results have been published. What I believe from my own experience working with online students and online faculty is that students need the involvement of their instructors in a classroom setting.

Class discussions provide an opportunity for transformational learning and that is a component often eliminated with these types of programs. Perhaps the answer lies somewhere in the middle, with a hybrid approach that blends classes and competencies as methods of measurement. Or perhaps the use of competencies could replace the traditional learning objectives as the basis for development of online courses.

I cannot predict with certainty how higher education will continue to evolve; however, I can state that students need interactions with their instructors. The role of the online instructor should not be minimized to that of a grader or evaluator alone as it results in missed learning opportunities and makes distance learning feel distant once again. I am an advocate for instructors developing a strong virtual presence and being highly involved with and responsive to their online students.

Through these interactions learning is transformative and becomes a process that is nurtured rather than a function to be completed. Through an instructor's involvement students are prompted to develop important skills, such as critical thinking, and they can help provide the context necessary to make learning meaningful and relevant.

What it Means to
Create an Online Learning Environment

Online education has been well-established and continues to sustain progress. In addition, online classes have been popular, even among traditional colleges, and there is still ongoing growth. While there is a focus on technology the basics of adult education do not change. The question then becomes of matter of whether or not learning conditions can be created by or enhanced through the use of technology.

For someone new to this environment they may also wonder if learning can take place and if so, how does an instructor adapt to this environment. The fundamental process of learning and knowledge acquisition doesn't change but the conditions have and this can either enhance or detract from students' developmental progress.

Creating an online course and adding students does not guarantee they will automatically learn. Online learning occurs as a result of the conditions an instructor establishes and nurtures, along with the interactions they develop with their students.

A Technology Enabled Environment

Over time the use of technology in higher education has become prevalent, with phrases such as hybrid classes and a flipped classroom indicating the continued evolution of traditional education. It is not a matter of just using technology to create a course, it depends upon the ability of students to interact with and utilize the technological tools. The number of schools offering online classes and degree programs has created a large base of students. This means that for-profit universities no longer hold a significant market advantage.

What educators find in a standard online classroom is a place for resources, a gradebook, a place for discussions, and other features such as course announcements. The classroom interface has also evolved over time and many learning management systems (LMS) providers offer easier navigation tools and resources to create a better user experience, along with data analytic tools for instructors.

Challenges for Instructors

One of the first challenges centers on who is responsible for ensuring that learning takes place in a virtual classroom. For example, can a curriculum developer set up a course shell and create an atmosphere that is certain to prompt learning? Of course the answer is no because it requires a human element.

Another challenge is that the instructor must become an active participant - from the first post made to interactions that occur with students. If an instructor maintains an active presence it will help to set the stage for learning to occur. If the instructor is not active or paying attention to class conditions, it will have a direct, negative affect on students and their ongoing development.

Even if class conditions are optimal, students must also be involved in and receptive to the learning process. Students must learn how to utilize the tools and resources that have been made available to them. In addition, instructors and students must learn to work together. Through my work as an online educator one of the most common complaints I hear is that the online class can feel mechanical in nature and new students who are not academically prepared can get overwhelmed and disengage from the class. This poses another challenge for educators as not all students are suited for this type of environment.

Creating Optimal Conditions

For an online class, technology establishes the environment and then technological tools are added based upon the course design. An instructor is assigned, students are added, and class begins.

What transforms this environment so that it becomes productive?

Instructors are given a checklist of facilitation duties and meeting those requirements will ensure the class runs according to plan. The test for instructors is in the specifics of those assigned duties.

For example, with class discussions there are a specific number of posts that are often required of the instructor and the purpose is to engage them in a dialogue with students. Those posts need to stimulate students' thought processes and curiosity, while connecting course concepts to real life. In addition, feedback is not just about a grade - although it is an indicator of progress being made. The purpose of feedback is to engage students in the content, add corrective comments to address developmental needs, and provide an itemization of the points earned.

Engaging Students in the Process

Classroom conditions involve what an instructor is actively doing. Engagement is about the content and effectiveness of interactions. For discussion question posts, consider how you address the student, invite the class to join in the conversation, acknowledge and validate their perspectives, add your expertise or experience, and then build a meaningful dialogue. For the feedback provided, develop comments for both the content of what was written and the mechanics. This is a teaching moment and if you provide feedback that matters, students are likely to start reading it week after week.

For communication with students, consider if you are viewed as approachable and responsive. This includes the tone that you take, which can be short and curt or warm, friendly, and helpful. In addition, be sure to respond to students in a timely manner so that you can alleviate their concerns. Never tell a student to "see the syllabus" as it is not very helpful and may deter them from further communication. Teach students where to look for information and encourage them so that you boost their confidence and engagement in the class.

Facilitation Strategies

An effective strategy for an online instructor is to develop an action plan and then conduct weekly self-reflection and self-assessment. An educator always has room to grow and improve. For new instructors it is helpful to develop a checklist of the basic course requirements. A seasoned instructor can break down tasks into specific days or time periods as they know it takes time and effort to nurture a class full of students.

Learning is not housed in an online classroom shell; it resides in the required activities and interactions between instructors and students. The basic rules of education apply - acquire information and knowledge, and then demonstrate what was learned and the progress made towards meeting course outcomes.

What has made online classes a better choice for many students is that they do more than memorize material for a test. There are authentic tasks such as written projects and required class participation that promotes learning. A course shell establishes a place for students to meet and resources to be acquired; however, it is purposeful, effective, and meaningful teaching that creates the conditions for learning to take place. Students who become motivated to participate in the process and immerse themselves in the discussions and required activities will find they can learn and grow, even with the use of technology.

Conditions that Promote Virtual Learning

Learning can be fun, engaging, and interesting, or it can seem dull, routine, and boring. This is true regardless of the format of the class, whether it occurs in a traditional or online classroom. It may also seem that learning online should be (or could be) just as effective as traditional classroom learning as the needs of the students are still the same.

In almost every online class, resources and materials are provided for students, there are asynchronous (and occasionally synchronous) discussions, and then assessments are given to determine if progress has been made with meeting the required learning objectives. Students aren't required to sit through a lecture and instead they can study at their own convenience. But important elements are missing in a virtual classroom, such as face to face interactions that provide visual and verbal cues, and that makes the distance factor a significant challenge.

So what can an instructor do to ensure that learning occurs in a virtual environment?

Most online classes contain a fairly standard structure, even with varying learning management systems, and many online schools provide pre-programmed courses for instructors to use that are developed with established learning objectives, course materials, and a variety of learning activities. However, creating a course and adding the content does not automatically guarantee that students are going to be engaged and learn something because of their required involvement.

Most experienced online instructors know that learning is a process that does not occur automatically and instead must be nurtured. Classroom learning is relational in nature and influenced by the environment an instructor develops, along with the interactions they have with their students.

Students and a Virtual Classroom

Consider the students' experience when they first enter a virtual classroom.

They need to navigate through the classroom, find the required materials, and become highly self-motivated to keep up with the discussions and assignments. Most learning management systems have evolved over time to make the user experience easier but the ability of a student to learn in this environment requires more than how they are able use the technological tools. In a traditional class students know exactly where they need to be and they are able to receive immediate assistance. They also interact with other students and develop a sense of community or being part of the class.

Learning is likely to occur when students feel connected to their class, believe the course will meet their academic and/or career needs, are able to obtain assistance when needed, and begin to develop productive working relationships with their instructors.

What can hinder this process and reduce the potential for learning is the reliance on written words as the primary form of communication. The classroom can then become almost perfunctory in nature for students and discourage them from being fully engaged and working towards peak performance. That's when the role of the online instructor becomes even more important.

Instructors and a Virtual Classroom

Instructors have many responsibilities, from knowing the subject matter they are required to teach to managing the classroom efficiently and effectively. This includes completing required facilitation duties, participating in discussions, providing feedback, and managing relationships. But one of the most important responsibilities is creating an environment that encourages students to be involved.

It may seem challenging to think about nurturing conditions like this in a virtual class but it is possible through an active instructional presence with an instructor who is highly involved and engaged in the class. This level of involvement allows students to "see" their instructor and this creates a perception that they care about the class.

There are factors that can work against an instructor, from a poorly designed course to a lack of engaging resources, which may not be easily corrected. Even if the classroom has been perfectly constructed an instructor must still be actively present and proactively working to create a positive experience for students.

It can be easy for students to withdraw and eventually disengage from an online class, which means an instructor must always be alert to changes in involvement and participation. This also speaks to the nature of learning, which can be easy for some students and challenging for others, especially if they lack fundamental academic skills.

5 Strategies to Create Optimal Conditions

As an instructor you cannot tell students to learn or expect that it will occur naturally. What you can do is to utilize strategies that prompt learning. The role of an instructor matters just as much as the design of the course and the materials provided. Students still need someone to encourage them and help them to connect with information in a meaningful manner so that learning occurs.

I have been actively involved in online faculty development and discovered that a majority of instructors can effectively manage their class and meet the required expectations. What I have also found is that approximately 25% of the instructors I've worked with perform above and beyond the minimal requirements, just as I have always tried to do as an online educator, to exceed the minimum requirements and create an engaging environment.

While it may seem that these strategies should be used by all instructors, some prefer to complete only what is required and while that is acceptable it does not lead to an optimal learning experience.

#1. Develop Engaging Discussion Posts:

Most online classes have some form of discussions, typically each week of the class. The requirements for instructors usually involve a specific number of days that they are to required respond to students and the quality of those posts may or may not be specifically stated in their contract. What an instructor's discussion response can do is to engage students in the topic, expand upon what they have written, prompt critical thinking and a deeper understanding of the course topics, and help students connect the topics to real world situations and issues.

An instructor's posts provide relevant context for the topics, if they are well developed. What can be added to the instructional posts is the instructor's professional experience, relevant insight, and acknowledgement that validates the effort made by students. The challenge is taking the time to craft responses that accomplish these goals and it requires being able to post something more than a quick reactive response. Try to acknowledge something that each student has written, then build from it in some manner, and conclude with a question that prompts their intellectual curiosity. When a post is substantive and engaging the dialogue with students is likely to continue.

#2. Be a Facilitator, Educator, and Teacher:

The work of an online instructor has been referred to by many names, including facilitator, educator, and teacher. While some online schools prefer the word facilitator, the work that an instructor performs involves much more than facilitating a process. A teacher is someone who can help students acquire the necessary academic skills and have the patience necessary to guide and direct them as they work towards improvement of their developmental needs. An educator is someone who understands the basics of adult learning and knows some of the theories that can inform their work.

To state that an instructor is a "guide on the side" seems to imply a passive role, while the development of a learning environment requires active rather than passive involvement. As instructors develop their knowledge base about adult education they are transformed and become an educator. Some faculty are hired because of their subject matter expertise but that does not automatically guarantee they can be effective as an instructor.

When an instructor is able to facilitate, educate, and teach, their effectiveness in the classroom becomes apparent in all aspects of their work.

#3. Provide Feedback That Prompts Reflection:

Instructors know that students need more than a letter grade to prompt their continued development and this aligns with the premise of self-directed adult learners who want to be involved in the learning process. Students want to know why they earned the grade received.

If they use grades as their primary source of motivation it becomes important to teach them to focus on more than their grades and instead understand the meaning of those grades and what can be learned from it. To do this the feedback needs to address the content of what was written, along with the mechanics, and be done in a manner that encourages their progress.

What some instructors rely upon, typically when there is little time available, is canned comments or quickly written commentary. Feedback is most effective when it causes students to become further interested in the topics and more importantly, when they reflect upon their work and academic progress. When students are engaged in the feedback process they are more likely to be responsive to what their instructor provides and learn from it.

#4. Be Actively Present and Engaged:

There is a misconception that an instructor cannot help students if they cannot see them. But an instructor can bridge the distance gap and create conditions that are conducive to learning. What I've learned through my online teaching experience, and background working with faculty, is that students can easily disengage from the class and if it isn't noticed right away it may be too late to encourage them to try again.

There are many reasons why students disengage and it may not be easy to know exactly why when working in a virtual classroom. For example, when students become frustrated or lose motivation they may begin to slowly withdraw and if an instructor is actively present they will notice the absence of those students.

What I've also observed is that student performance is often directly influenced by the level of engagement of the instructor. An instructor's virtual presence is also a social presence that builds a sense of community among students that helps keep them engaged and interested in the class.

#5. Develop Effective Communication Techniques:

The primary form of communication in an online classroom consists of written posts and messages. Interactions and relationships in a virtual class are also based upon written words. At first this may seem to be an impersonal form of communication because of the many potential issues that can arise.

A challenge that is present will all messages and posts is that those forms of communication are subject to interpretation, along with a perceived tone and intent of the message posted. Since messages are sent asynchronously it means that the instructor is not present to ensure the message was interpreted correctly. While written words are not the most effective method of communication it is still possible for students to develop a positive perception about the instructor's disposition towards helping them.

This is a reminder that anything an instructor decides to post needs to be done from a position of care and concern, rather than from feelings of frustration or an emotional response and reaction. When coaching online faculty, I've made a suggestion to create posts first, perhaps in a Word document, as that will help to manage the mechanics and tone of what is written.

If a negative emotional reaction is experienced during class, perhaps as a reaction to something a student has written or posted, it would be better to delay any form of a response until it can be approached from a logical and rational perspective. This helps with the development of productive working relationships and models effective communication for students to follow.

Teach Students the Potential for Distance Learning

An instructor's involvement, which is their active online presence, influences how students respond to the virtual classroom environment, how well they perform, engage in the class, and stay motivated. What I've learned through working with faculty is that the online classroom comes to life when instructors are involved in all aspects of the class in a meaningful manner. Classroom management is not just a matter of overseeing what takes place but being an active participant and engaging students with all roles performance.

Every instructional task is important and all communication matters. The work an instructor does as an educator, teacher, and facilitator, also determines how effective the learning process will be. The development of conditions that are conducive to learning needs to be nurtured every week, until the class concludes. Once a new class starts, the need for developing the same type of environment begins again.

Just as learning is never a one-time event, so too is the art and skill of online teaching. Students will learn best when they are in an environment that encourages them to do so and this is in direct control of their instructors.

How to Create Online Group Work

The online classroom presents unique challenges and opportunities for the process of learning. One of the challenges that instructors need to address is how to promote collaboration among students in this type of environment. Discussion boards are utilized within most online classrooms as a means of replicating the traditional classroom model of interactive discussions. The question for instructors is whether or not participation within discussion question threads is enough to promote collaboration and a sense of community.

There is another alternative that could be implemented and it is the use of group work. Creating group assignments may not seem like a natural fit for a technologically enabled learning environment; however, there are benefits that could be realized if the right conditions are established.

Benefits of Group Work

Many students who take online classes are considered to be non-traditional students or working adults, which means they generally understand the importance of taking responsibility for their work. Class discussions provide them with an opportunity to interact and share their ideas, knowledge, ideas, and experiences.

The development of group projects or assignments can enhance this interactive learning process by requiring students to work together to produce a written assignment or contribute to a project, one that requires the group to reach a conclusion about a current issue or solve a relevant problem through new ideas and solutions.

The use of group assignments has additional benefits for students when they utilize skills that are necessary for their academic and professional development, including communication, negotiation, compromise, delegation, project management, and consensus-building skills.

Students may also use advanced cognitive functions such as critical thinking skills while involved in group work when they are challenged to make individual contributions and evaluate alternative solutions. Students are likely to become more involved in the process when they find the work is applicable to their career or other professional interests.

Creating a Structure for Group Work

A challenge for the implementation of group assignments in an online environment results from the lack of face-to-face interaction, which can affect the level of participation in the group. A common method of addressing this issue is to have group members sign a team contract that holds each student accountable for equal participation and contributions to the project.

There may be initial resistance from students who do not like to work in a group setting because of prior experiences or their preferred learning style. It becomes important then to explain the purpose and potential benefits of group work, while also helping students find ways of interacting that are convenient to their schedule.

For example, students may use synchronous technology tools such as instant messaging or live chat as a means of working together. Students can also utilize asynchronous forms of communication such as e-mail and threads that are posted within the classroom.

Forms of Group Work

The most basic form of group work is a written assignment, which can be a case study, research paper, or analysis. Other forms of group work that may be more interesting for students to complete include the development of a group wiki, blog, or portfolio. Those types of assignments provide an instructor with a better opportunity to monitor the progress of each group, instead of waiting until the due date to ascertain if the group has completed a paper and done so in a manner that meets all of the requirements, provided that groups are required to complete the project in phases.

The Instructor's Role

One of the most important aspects for the successful development of group projects is the role the instructor takes in the process. An instructor needs to provide a working time line, project deadlines, and learning objectives; while establishing ground rules and expectations. A proactive approach to facilitation of group work includes providing direction, guidance, and feedback throughout the entire development of the group and their deliverables. An instructor also needs to know when to intervene when there are disputes or conflicts that the group itself cannot resolve.

Overall, group work can contribute to the interactive process of adult learning by encouraging students to utilize skills that are relevant to their academic and professional development. This can be accomplished in an online classroom if the instructor establishes an environment that is conducive to collaboration and teamwork.

End of Chapter Check-In

What Have You Learned?

What Are Your Strengths?

What Are Your Developmental Areas?

What Will You Apply to Your Teaching Practice?

CHAPTER 5.
ONLINE CLASS DISCUSSIONS

How to Help Students Engage in Discussions

Class discussions can be very rewarding but also time-consuming for an instructor in any learning environment. This is especially true for educators when there is a large class-size, complex course topics, the instructor is an adjunct and has other responsibilities, or it is the first time an instructor has taught the course.

There are two possible options available when an instructor is faced with the demands of facilitating a discussion and the first is to go through the motions and meet the minimal require-ments needed to facilitate the class. From my experience working with online faculty that approach usually results in posts that appear to be talking at students, rather than trying to engage them in a conversation, and telling them what they need to know instead of prompting them to explore the topics further.

The other instructional option, one that is likely to be more successful, is to devote the time necessary to be actively involved in the ongoing conversations. This includes prep time or developing talking points for the instructional posts prior to the start of class.

Regardless of the option chosen as an instructional strategy, class discussions need the instructor's active engagement and involvement so that students remain focused on the topic and actively engaged in the class discussions.

An Instructor Sets the Tone

During any class discussion it is the instructor who sets the tone and models what it means to be present and fully engaged in an ongoing and productive conversation.

Students look at their instructor's involvement for guidance and feedback, especially when they are struggling with articulating their thoughts or working with the required subject matter. An instructor that posts well-developed and well-researched participation messages, or has provided thoughtful discussion prompts, will add in supplemental resources and share their experience so that the topics come to life and are applicable to the real world.

Since this can be a time-consuming process instructors need a strategy to make the process both manageable and meaningful. Instructors can cultivate engaging online class discussions with the use of process I've called guided ANCHORS.

Developing Discussions with ANCHORS

The first step in developing ANCHORS is to **Acknowledge** a student's post in some manner, whether it is their attempt to answer the discussion question or their perspective of the topic.

The next step involves **Nurturing** their development by being supportive when responding, rather than calling them out on something they have written.

The third step is to respond in a manner that prompts their **Critical** thinking about the subject. This can involve taking the course materials and guiding them through the process of analysis, synthesis, and application to the real world. The inclusion of questions is one of the most effective methods of prompting the development of critical thinking skills.

The next step is to **Highlight** important points in the course materials and address any aspect of the readings that students are struggling with as they post their responses.

The fifth step in the process of developing ANCHORS is to take an **Organized** approach to the development of instructional responses. Instructional participation posts and discussion prompts should not be reactive responses. Instead those posts should be carefully crafted and developed in a manner that builds from what the students have stated or posted.

This leads into the next step and that is the inclusion of **Research** and/or supplemental sources to strengthen the instructor's responses. The last step is to create a **Springboard** or post follow up questions that help to further the conversation. A response that simply acknowledges something the student has written, or provides professional expertise without a specific context, may not be enough to create an ongoing discussion.

Instructional Strategy

The use of ANCHORS as an instructional strategy can be done to enhance your current approach to class participation and it can also serve as a means of critiquing what you currently post or have prepared for your facilitation of the class.

To make your contributions more meaningful you may want to consider your students' perspective of the discussions and keep in mind they are trying their best to respond and be engaged. If the subject is too difficult and there is no active instructional presence or meaningful contributions during the class, students may disengage from the discussions.

Utilizing ANCHORS is also helpful when you have a new class, a subject you have never taught before, or a topic that does not align with your professional background.

The development of substantive instructional responses takes time and practice. It also requires the development of an effective time management plan. Every message posted in an online discussion represents your level of commitment to the learning process. When you respond to your students, consider their needs and the purpose of the discussion.

Develop ANCHORS to make the process of instructional participation more engaging and meaningful, which can also help you when a discussion may not be appealing or interesting from your own perspective. This process will allow you to encourage, nurture, challenge, and support your students' progress and development. When class discussions are engaging all students can benefit and have a potential to learn from it.

How to Engage the Mind of Your Students

The ideal outcome for any class, whether it is a traditional college course or online class, is to have students demonstrate they are able to meet the course objectives, which could include the acquisition of new knowledge or the development of specific skills that are academic and/or career related.

Yet the reality for many classes is that some students will appear to go through the motions without actually learning anything, even if they have written a paper, participated in the class discussions to some degree, or passed a required exam.

What experienced educators know is that learning takes place not just in the classroom but within the mind of their students and that is where the focus of educating adults needs to begin - on the mindset, attitude, and mental capacity that every student has while they are participating in class and working through the course materials.

The optimal class conditions could be well established and the best materials provided yet there are students who still do not connect with the class or course concepts. Active involvement by students does not always occur automatically, it requires guided instruction through all aspects of the class and with all learning activities. A highly involved instructor is needed to work with students and monitor their progress to ensure that they are not just present but their minds are fully engaged in the learning process.

The Mind of an Adult Student

Cognition is a word that refers to how the mind receives and processes information. The mind is in control of the flow of information and knowledge, which must always be a consideration when a course is developed and delivered to students. The classroom conditions and environment established by the instructor will determine the initial perception and mindset students develop about their course. This means that students will either begin from a mindset of being willing or resistant to being involved.

Once the class has begun and materials are provided, they are initially passive recipients of that information. The method in which the course was designed and the content is delivered will have a direct impact on how their mind is engaged and the information is received, processed, and filtered. Other factors such as attention span, focus, and academic preparedness will further influence their mental capabilities or cognition.

Initially when information is received the mind stores it in working memory, which has a limited capacity as to how much it can hold. When there is a lot of material to review or process there may be a point when the mind filters out and discards some of the information. The purpose of a class is not just to give students knowledge about a subject but work to ensure that it is retained in long-term memory.

This requires students to engage their mind in the subject being studied and place the information in a context that is relevant to their existing knowledge, background, and experience. If class discussions and learning activities are successful in helping students retain knowledge it then becomes stored, categorized, and organized in long-term memory, which means it can be recalled and utilized at a later time.

The Context for Learning

When a college class is developed it is meant to provide students with the right amount of information, materials, and resources; along with planned activities that are designed to encourage students to be involved in the learning process. However, it is not uncommon for students to finish a class and forget a significant amount of knowledge acquired, if there was no consideration given as to how students will process the information they have been given. This means they must transform from passive to active learners as they are involved in class, if they are going to retain information in long term memory.

While this is partially a matter of how the course was designed, which can be beyond the control of most instructors, the method of delivery can also have an impact on the retention of knowledge related to course subjects and topics. The role of an instructor is to provide a context for the course concepts and help students work with it so they are able to understand, comprehend, relate to, and connect with it in a meaningful manner.

Leading the Learning Process

The words instructor, teacher, and facilitator are used almost interchangeably for educators. Teaching often refers to primary school educators yet it can also apply to higher education as an instructor must still be responsible for direct involvement with students in the learning process.

There is a trend in higher education to de-emphasize a teacher-led approach, especially for online schools, yet instructors still have a subject they need to teach through their feedback and instructional posts. Facilitation applies to any classroom environment as it describes the role of an instructor as someone who is facilitating a learning process.

Regardless of the word that is used to describe an instructor's role within a classroom environment, a student-centered, teacher-led, instructional approach is still required because students need to be prompted to engage their advanced cognitive functions.

Strategies to Engage the Mind

Learning occurs as a result of a willing and engaged mind. An instructor who wants to promote learning can do so by employing any one or all of the strategies provided below as a means of encouraging cognitive development. These methods apply to traditional or online classes as learning takes place first within the mind of the students.

Learn Your Subject Matter Well:

If an instructor only has a cursory understanding of the subject matter they are teaching it will be much more difficult to provide a relevant context and help engage students in the topics. With the availability of online sources for any given subject matter an instructor can stay current in their field and strengthen the facilitation of their class.

Share Your Relevant Professional Experience

Providing professional stories and examples is a very helpful method of showing what the course topics mean for a particular industry or type of business, and it allows an instructor to use the textbook as a springboard for learning. A helpful suggestion would be to scan the materials and topics for the upcoming week and write down examples that are ready for the discussions.

Explore the Textbook and Consider Additional Sources

A textbook will provide foundational concepts to build upon, along with elements such as examples, case studies, questions, problems, etc. Those are tools that can be utilized during class discussions or as supplemental activities as a means of working through the topics. It is also possible that additional sources will be useful when current examples and case studies are needed. An instructor can look ahead at the upcoming class week and prepare a bank of sources and notes that can be utilized as needed during the discussions.

Encourage Guided Discussion

A class discussion is the heart of any class, in any learning environment, as it can engage the mind and prompt further thinking about the course subjects. This is a time when students can explore the topics and interact with other students, provided that they are encouraged to do so in a safe and welcoming environment.

There are several inherent challenges with class discussions and the first is encouraging students to post messages when some may naturally shy away from conversations, which requires prompting them to be involved. The second challenge is keeping students on topic and this is a balancing act that instructors address by carefully guiding the direction of the discussions. When students do participate they become actively involved by working with concepts rather than just reading about them.

Provide Meaningful Feedback

When a paper has been submitted that is poorly written, contains numerous mechanical errors, or has over-utilized sources to create the content, it can be challenging to follow the thought process used by the student and much easier to focus on writing mistakes.

However, a majority of students who submit a paper have made an effort and that is what needs to be analyzed. This provides an instructor with an opportunity to further interact with their students about the course topics and provide feedback that prompts their thinking and strengthens their analysis. It becomes important then to allow enough time each week to carefully read through their papers and provide comments that encourages students to reflect upon and learn from the feedback provided.

Any instructional strategy used must be done with the purpose of helping students connect with information received in a manner that promotes comprehension through interaction, application through context, and retention in long-term memory for future recall. Regardless of the tools and instructional methods used, the learning process takes time. This is why it becomes necessary to help students become involved in class and guide them as they work with the subjects.

While the manner in which a course was designed can promote or inhibit learning, it is the internal cognitive processes that ultimately determine what students learn and retain. The critical component for any class is the instructor's level of involvement. While mental functions cannot be seen or the internalized processes evaluated, an instructor can help students become mentally engaged and actively involved as they interact with and guide them throughout the class.

Managing Diversity in Online Classes

The online classroom is a diverse mix of students with different backgrounds, experiences, cultures, and characteristics because students are not confined to one particular geographic location. While this certainly sounds exciting it can also be a new experience for many students. This virtual environment can promote collaboration as well as confrontation or conflict. It is important not to manage diversity but the interactions and online classroom conditions for the benefit of producing meaningful exchanges.

Ground Rules Are Necessary

One of the starting points for instructors to take is to establish ground rules for online communication, which is often referred to the Rules of Netiquette. The basic premise of these guidelines are to promote respectful posts between students while they interact with each other.

Keep in mind that effective online classroom management requires much more. It is an ongoing process of monitoring posts, taking corrective action when necessary, and modeling proper communication. If students are new to this type of environment they will need coaching and guidance as they learn these crucial skills.

Keep Discussions on Track

Where this all begins is with the online discussions. Most online schools have a mandatory participation requirement and that means students must interact with each other. It is easy for these discussions to turn into opinion-based posts rather than well-researched academic responses. When that occurs it presents an opportunity for students to voice their beliefs, which may be in direct conflict with other students' beliefs. At that point the discussion may veer off track and emotional reactions occur.

Instructors can help prevent this from taking place through their continual interaction and feedback with responsive posts. When students are prompted to utilize higher cognitive functions and move away from posts that are reactive in nature they learn to view discussions as a place for intellectual discourse. Of course the students' background and experiences are relevant; however, it needs to be shaped through an objective rather than subjective lens. As students implement critical thinking skills they begin to take a broader view and consider real-world perspectives.

Leverage Collaboration

Class discussions also have an ability to promote collaborative efforts when students believe that they are working with each other. This cannot be accomplished through forced compliance rather it happens as students begin to develop a sense of community among each other. One way to start this process is through classroom introductions, which allow students to view each other as real people. This also allows instructors to gauge students' reactions to each other and learn more about their background.

There are varying levels of diversity within online classes and in reality, instructors may not know the extent of their students' diverse qualities because they are not physically present. The most effective approach for managing a diverse class is to encourage all students to contribute to the discussions and create conditions that promote interactions in a safe and respectable manner. All students have something unique to share simply because of their life experiences. Teach them to ask questions, model the process, and intervene when signs of conflict occur. It is likely that all students have something to learn and they will benefit from diverse viewpoints.

End of Chapter Check-In

What Have You Learned?

What Are Your Strengths?

What Are Your Developmental Areas?

What Will You Apply to Your Teaching Practice?

CHAPTER 6.
STUDENT-CENTERED STRATEGIES

How Do You Nurture
a Supportive Approach to Instruction?

As an instructor, are you aware of how your students are performing at all times?

Do you maintain a proactive or reactive approach to instruction?

It is possible that you have developed a routine for your instructional tasks and address students when they ask questions or submit assignments. However, there is an aspect of teaching that requires your continued commitment and that is the manner in which you interact with and support your students.

Every educator is aware of the challenges involved in trying to create a dynamic and engaging learning environment, one that is supportive of the learning process and the developmental needs of students. Adjuncts face a greater challenge, especially those who are teaching online classes, as they do not have an opportunity to meet with students face-to-face on a regular basis. The time required to prepare instructional materials, along with completing other tasks such as meaningful feedback, is significant and it can be easy to lose sight of the perspective of your students when there are many instructional tasks that need to be completed.

One perspective of my students that I am always concerned with is how they are adapting to the classroom environment and responding to the required learning tasks. As an educator I want to be supportive of their development, especially when it involves changing behaviors or habits. Students rely upon habits and patterns of working in a particular manner to meet the requirements of each class, and the idea of having to perform differently in some form can create a mental roadblock or barrier to their progress. Students may also not recognize a need to make changes in how they work or perform until it has been brought to their attention through feedback or interactions in class, and they may or may not be willing to accept it - unless I have established a productive working relationship with them.

While every instructor has many aspects of classroom management to consider, and focusing on students individually at all times may not be a priority, there are instructional practices that can be implemented that will assist students and create a supportive approach to instruction.

Learning Requires Adapting

Maintaining a supportive approach is needed as learning requires adapting. Instructors expect students to perform in a uniform manner, which means they must learn to follow the academic guidelines, adhere to school policies, and complete what is expected of them within the time frames established.

As instructors know, not all students are fully prepared to work in a productive manner or have all of the academic skills necessary to perform their best. That means these students will have to learn to adapt and make changes as needed.

There will be students, especially new students, who need to adapt in some manner to these expectations and requirements, which means making changes to how they think, behave, or respond. The transition made from one class to the next requires adapting to a new instructor, new expectations, new students, and possibly new procedures. Students also experience change as part of learning as they may need to adapt what they believe and even what they know about course subjects or topics. Students are more likely to adapt if they feel supported by their instructors.

Students Who Are Self-Directed

The principle of adult education that explains how adults learn is known as andragogy, and it holds that adults are independent and self-directed in their ability to be involved in the learning process. That doesn't always mean they know what to do or what is best for them. For example, if I were to ask a group of students to tell me what they need to work on or their most critical developmental needs - they may or may not be able to accurately articulate what is needed unless they were to refer back to feedback I've provided.

The next consideration is whether or not that self-directed nature helps or inhibits their ability to adapt and change when needed. What often occurs is that it can create initial resistance if they believe they know best about their ability to learn or they disagree with feedback received from their instructor. The attitude that a self-directed adult student holds is directly influenced by the relationship they have established with their instructors, which can be productive or adversarial.

Supportive Instructional Strategies

An instructor's approach has an impact on how students respond when they interact with them. For example, if the tone of feedback or communication is stern or threatening, students may feel intimidated and not respond well. As another example, if students start a new class and find their instructor has different expectations of them, it can create resistance - especially if they have been working in the same manner in past classes and received positive outcomes.

As a result, students may have emotional or reactive responses, express their feelings tactfully or otherwise, or they may quietly withdraw and disengage from their class, if they are not supported by their instructors. What follows are strategies that an instructor can implement to nurture a supportive approach to instruction.

#1. Provide Supportive Feedback

The learning process is also a behavioral process that occurs through a series of progressive steps. The first step is to comprehend and understand what they are going to do, why they are going to complete the required tasks, and determine if they have the resources and skills needed to complete what is required.

When feedback is received and developmental areas have been noted, students have to make a decision whether they will accept or reject it. An instructor will be more effective if they can relate these developmental needs to the potential for positive outcomes and improved performance.

Consider this perspective of learning, especially for a new student: The first attempt a student makes to complete a required task is usually the most important step in the process. If they experience positive outcomes, such as encouragement or improved results, they will likely try it again. However, if they make an attempt and experience a negative outcome, such as criticism or a lack of an acknowledgement from their instructor, they may stop, give up, quit, or disengage from class.

#2. Prepare Students to Adapt

If you are going to propose that students try to do something new or different, help prepare them before they begin. This includes offering resources or creating an action plan with them so they know the steps to take. This creates a roadmap that sets them up for success. You can establish checkpoints along the way as a means of providing follow-up and checking in with them on their progress, so they feel supported.

If the suggested changes were noted in their feedback, offer to have a follow-up conversation with them to clarify the purpose and intent of your feedback. You will also find it helpful to be available to answer any questions they may have as that extra effort helps to build a connection. This is especially important with online classes as that they cannot "see" you in a virtual environment.

The most important advice I can offer is to never give up on students, even when they want to quit. Some students need a nudge or put in extra effort to get past mental barriers or a lack of self-confidence.

#3. Focus on Strengths, Not Deficits

I've found that one of the most effective and engaging methods of working with students is taking an approach that is focused on their strengths rather than their deficits. For example, I've used the sandwich approach to feedback. It begins by noting something positive, then addresses developmental issues, and concludes with another positive aspect - even if the only positive aspect of their performance is acknowledging the effort they have made.

The more you encourage the effort that students have made, the better that effort is likely to become in the long run. You can share details that outline how you have assessed their performance and if there are many issues to address, try selecting the most important or critical issue first so they do not become overwhelmed. You want them to view the process of learning as something that is done through incremental steps. And if you believe that students don't read and implement feedback provided, be sure to make yours meaningful and ask follow up questions as a means of creating a dialogue with them.

Develop Positive Beliefs

The duration of most college classes provides instructors with a limited amount of time to get to know their students and work with them. Most instructors may not develop a true sense of the potential of their students until they have had time to interact with them and review their performance.

It is unlikely that an instructor will know about prior feedback students have received, or if their performance has improved or declined from their prior classes. I've learned to focus on how students are performing now and never assume they don't know better, they aren't trying, or they haven't been making any improvements. I always believe that all students have a capacity to learn and my approach to instruction determines how well they will respond and perform.

To create a supportive instructional approach, focus on the specifics of what students need to improve upon in a manner that encourages their progress. This will demonstrate to your students that you have their best interests in mind. If you expect students to adapt to your personal preferences and they do not see the benefits of trying what you've suggested, you may find yourself at odds with them. Every student has a potential to try something new and make changes; however, it often becomes a matter of whether or not they see the benefits of implementing your suggestions or trying to meet your expectations.

Your relationship with students, along with your disposition about their development, will go a long way towards helping them adapt and discover that ongoing development is a natural part of the learning process. When you nurture a supportive approach to your instruction, you will also nurture a positive mindset in your students.

Developing Student-Centered Strategies

Distance learning is known for its successes and its challenges. When the online classroom environment fails to connect with students it results in low engagement and retention in the class. What works best is an environment that stimulates an interest in learning and promotes meaningful interactions.

Who has the greatest influence when it comes to the type of class environment that is experienced, the students or their instructor? Of course it is the instructor who establishes conditions and students in turn respond or react to what they perceive as they are involved in the class, along with what they actually experience as they interact with their instructor and other students.

It is ultimately an instructor's responsibility to create conditions that promote learning and active involvement, regardless of the learning management system and technological tools that have been (or not been) utilized. Many of the online instructors I've worked with through my role as a faculty development specialist, especially newer instructors, become focused on the required contractual obligations first and that can take a majority of their time if they are working as an adjunct and have other full time responsibilities.

The traditional format for teaching in higher education is instructor-led, which means the instructor dictates how and what students must learn. For online classes there is a trend among schools to have the courses pre-developed for instructors, leaving little flexibility for them to make changes or enhancements What this can do is to create a mindset that approaches instruction as a function rather than a process that can be nurtured.

When instructors see an online classroom that is already set up and the materials have been pre-loaded it creates a mindset for many that they have no control over the learning process. It is often a subconscious thought process and I certainly understand from my own experience what it's like to look at a class and only feel that you are there to grade papers and/or be involved in class discussions.

What is needed with all online classes, regardless of who develops the class, are student-centered instructional strategies that help to involve and engage students in the learning process. This requires a conscious effort and focus by instructors to be an active participant in the process and use interactions, communication, and feedback (the elements they have control over) to encourage learning.

Online Students and Learning

A challenge for establishing a student-centered approach to online teaching is the absence of face-to-face exchanges that humanize the learning experience for both instructors and students. This can lead to students feeling as if they are on their own, until they develop a connection with their instructors.

Students are constantly challenged to be adaptive to changes in their classes, work with different instructors, learn new procedures, and develop new methods of studying and learning. Instructors cannot see their students to gauge how they are progressing in class, which means they must be on the lookout for virtual indicators as students are actively involved in the learning process.

Instructors who are not monitoring the involvement level of their class may soon find students who have disengaged after it is too late to initiate a successful intervention.

Student-Centered Online Learning

What makes it challenging for instructors to maintain a student-centered approach in the long run is the time required to go above and beyond the mandatory instructional duties. Anyone who has taught an online course knows that it is challenging to balance the instructional requirements, such as deadlines for feedback, while maintaining a focus on each student's individual developmental progress.

For an adjunct this time challenge becomes even greater because they are likely working full-time while teaching on a part-time basis. No matter what conditions the online instructor is working within they must always develop and maintain a student-centered mindset and approach towards teaching.

A student focus is not just about putting every student first while balancing other responsibilities - it also involves considering their progress and development as they are involved in all of the required learning activities, including written assignments. This means that an instructor must be monitoring class conditions on a regular basis, receptive to student questions or concerns, and responsive to every virtual interaction.

An instructor who decides to only meet the minimum instructional requirements will likely find that level of instruction is not going to be enough to produce a student-centered focus, one that encourages individualized learning and provides personalized feedback.

Student-Centered and Student-Focused Strategies

The basic premise of student-centered teaching is the development of different learning types, which includes active learning (getting students involved) and cooperative learning (students are interacting with each other). These approaches to learning can be expanded upon to create student-focused instructional strategies.

#1. Prompt Student Engagement:

This applies to their participation in discussions and involvement in the class. During class discussions, try to respond to every student at least once and when you do, ask direct follow-up questions that help to promote their higher order or critical thinking skills. Students that are new to the learning process may report what they've read and/or add a general opinion about the topic instead of providing an in-depth analysis.

Your involvement can help guide their thought processes and encourage them to expand upon what they've written. If you see that students are not involved in the discussions, or there are some who are absent from class, reach out and check in with them.

#2. Encourage the Effort Made by Your Students:

When you provide feedback for assignments and learning activities, try the sandwich method approach and start with something positive. Then address a developmental need and conclude with a positive statement. If you have students who are struggling, you can always encourage them based upon the effort made as that will determine if they will continue to make an attempt. If they are doing what they perceive is their best and only receive negative feedback, they can easily get discouraged and give up.

A common feedback challenge for instructors involves reviewing papers that are poorly written and have numerous errors with spelling, grammar, formatting, and other mechanical issues. I've seen many instructors focus on the mechanics of the paper to the point where the content was overlooked or barely addressed.

This can be very frustrating for a student that has spent time trying to understand and write about the course topics and more importantly, wants to learn. The feedback process provides another opportunity for an instructor to teach and the students to learn.

#3. Encourage Reflection through Self-Assessment:

Sometimes it is helpful to find other methods of instructions to help students learn. One method that I've employed is the use of self-reflection techniques. If you can teach students to be reflective it will help them learn to self-assess their progress, and in time they can develop a sense of self-empowerment rather than believe that they have no control over their outcomes. The most common method of self-reflection is to use a journal, although many students may not find that to be an appealing option.

As an instructor you can also provide self-assessment techniques such as a one-minute paper that will help them review what they know about a subject. While the class may have an established structure already, and you are unable to add graded assignments, you could offer it as an option for those students who want to experience continued development and receive supplemental guidance.

This will take additional time on the part of the instructor as well as the students; however, for those students who accept the activity it can prove to be a valuable learning strategy. Through the use of reflection and self-assessment you can help students take ownership of their involvement in class and you will likely see improvement in their overall progress.

#4. Be an Example for Your Students:

As an online instructor you need to establish a highly visible and interactive virtual presence, which is also referred to as a social presence according to the Community of Inquiry framework. Being visibly present means that you are actively engaged in the class and class discussions, and in turn students develop a perception that you care about the class. Their level of involvement may increase because of what they perceive about your instructional presence and it will either be confirmed or discounted.

What I've found is that most instructors who are actively present in class are concerned about providing an extra level of attention for their students and the students are receptive to their responsiveness. I've always found that if I set an example as someone who is highly engaged in the class, my students follow that lead. You will likely find through your own instructional practice that students too will follow your lead and if you are active and responsive, there is a good possibility they will be too.

#5. Learn to Leverage Your Subject Matter Expertise:

Just because you take a student-focused approach it does not mean that you are going to sit idly by and watch the students interact. Your students will still need instruction and the benefit of your experience and expertise. You can share your knowledge through class discussions when you provide a real world context. You will likely have more industry experience than your students, although you should never rule out the possibility that students do have something of value to add - even with limited experience.

In addition, many online classes have students with a wide range of ages and that means you may have students in your class with extensive career experience, even though they have limited academic experience.

Regardless of the experience level of your students, you can weave in examples from your background that help to bring the course concepts to life. You can also add in your knowledge and expertise with weekly announcements, course posts, and written lectures. This helps guide students as they attempt to comprehend the course subjects and provides clarity for the course topics.

#6. Always Consider the Perspective of Your Students:

As you reflect upon the progress of your students, you can ask yourself:

What are their developmental needs? Are the instructions provided clear and concise? Is the feedback a true reflection of their progress and does it help guide their thinking about the topic they have written about or discussed?

It is easy to get to know the learning activities of your class well enough that you except students to respond or write in a certain manner and while this is helpful as a general rule, learning is an individualized process and it is influenced by the posts, materials, and resources you've provided - which needs to be reviewed by you on a regular basis.

When you provide feedback, think of students individually so you provide personalized guidance rather than canned general comments. I remember receiving what appeared to be canned comments as an online student and to me it seemed that the instructor either didn't care about my work or was too busy to provide meaningful feedback.

Student-Centered Learning Can Be Transformational

One of the underlying theories of adult education is called andragogy, which makes a distinction between teaching children (pedagogy) and adults. For adult students there is a need to be self-directed, which means they are directly involved and make decisions about their involvement in class. This translates into the online environment best when an instructor is student focused and implements student-centered strategies that are focused on the needs and development of their students.

What student centered teaching does is transform a virtual, distant environment into one that creates conditions conducive to active engagement, participation, and productive interactions. It depends upon instructors to take the time necessary to cultivate this approach to teaching, remembering that every strategy implemented must be connected to the needs of their students. When students are at the center of the learning process, they are transformed and the class is also transformed into an engaging and dynamic environment.

The Importance of Consistency in Teaching

If you were to ask students what they expect from you as an instructor, what would they state? Would they talk about your teaching style, level of communication, working relationship with them, responsiveness, or quality of feedback? An aspect of classroom facilitation that is expected from instructors but not frequently discussed among students is consistency. Students want a consistent learning environment and expect their instructors will create conditions that are conducive to productive exchanges.

What is Consistency?

What does consistency involve and what are the components of consistency that students talk about when they are sharing feedback with other students or completing an end of class evaluation? Consistency is the culmination of actions an instructor takes throughout the duration of the class, which has a direct impact on classroom interactions and the credibility of the instructor. While consistency cannot be measured in specific terms it is a general approach that can be practiced and monitored through self-reflection.

The most important aspect of consistency is action. This includes consistency in communication, tone, feedback, and classroom policies. When instructors are communicating with students there is a need for professionalism and emotional intelligence with the tone and content of all messages, on a consistent basis. Students also want to be able to rely upon their instructor to provide uniform and timely feedback that is focused on their academic well-being.

When Students Find Inconsistency

One area where students find inconsistent actions often involves the way that classroom policies and procedures are administered. For example, a student may request an exception to the late policy, expecting that their sincerity or unique circumstances will justify an exception. While an instructor may consider the request and have flexibility for extenuating circumstances, the overall impact of the final decision must be weighed as upholding consistent policies is essential for maintaining classroom order. The outcome of consistent or inconsistent actions is the credibility of the instructor.

Consider Your Instruction

As you reflect upon facilitation of your class, do you act based upon what you tell your students you will do? Do students perceive you as being reliable? The development of strong working relationships depends upon students believing that they can trust you and it is a product of interactions that occur over time. If you are responsive to the needs of your students, they will learn to trust your judgment and the guidance you offer. You can establish consistency by following through with your students and delivering what you promise, and later following up with them to ensure clarity and understanding.

As you model consistent behavior in the class you will find that you can also require this from your students. Instructors can expect students to exhibit behaviors that they embrace and model on a regular basis. Consistent actions promote effective teaching and establish efficient classroom operations.

Take Action When Students Aren't Engaged in Class

In a perfect classroom environment, every student would be engaged in the course, interested in the subjects, and performing to the very best of their capabilities. That's what every educator hopes for when they start teaching a class.

The reality for most classes is that while some students may be highly engaged and motivated, other students will base their involvement upon what is experienced in the classroom and whether or not their expectations are being met. While addressing student engagement can be challenging for traditional classroom educators, it can be even more difficult for online educators who cannot see their students or meet with them for a scheduled class time.

At the start of a new online class educators typically find that students are involved in the class with mixed feelings of excitement, apprehension, and uncertainty. From the perspective of a student, remaining motivated and engaged in the class requires substantial effort. While many students are self-directed in nature, and have an ability to sustain their involvement, there are often others who lack self-motivation and begin to disengage over time. As many educators realize, by the time a student disengages from class it is often too late to get them back on track.

A challenge for instructors is that online class facilitation can take a significant amount of time. With a busy schedule it is natural to focus on contractual obligations and classroom management, and not notice a student who is slowly disengaging from the class until they are completely absent or have withdrawn. It becomes important then to take a proactive approach with online students and establish an instructional approach for helping them to stay focused and engaged in the class.

Student Engagement Defined

When educators define the nature of student engagement it is usually done from a tangible (what is seen) perspective and this can be a subjective assessment. For example, if a student is posting participation online messages most every day of the week you might say they are highly engaged. The question is how active does a student have to be to meet this criteria? If they are posting messages on five days is that the same level of engagement as a student who is posting on six days?

As a general guideline it can be assessed by how invested students appear to be in their class. This includes their involvement in discussions, asking questions, submitting assignments on time, and how responsive they are to other students and their instructor. If a student is going to be considered highly engaged in class, an instructor needs to observe several visual cues.

Why Does Engagement Matter?

Engagement matters because it indicates that students are involved in the class. When students are fully engaged, a distance education class begins to feel like a community. If students are not actively involved in their class, especially an online class, they can easily disengage, lose interest, and eventually withdraw. If the instructor doesn't intervene, these students may drop the course and a continual pattern like this may also lead to disengagement from their degree program.

Visual cues are important then because they are indicators of how involved students are in the process of learning. These cues include qualities such as their level of effort, along with their responsiveness to feedback, communication, and coaching.

How to Measure Student Engagement

When visual cues are interpreted it is often done in a subjective manner, looking at more than a student's tangible work product or written papers. The purpose of measuring engagement in the class is to raise an educator's conscious awareness of students and keep track of their involvement.

It is easy to become so busy managing class operations and discussions that students who are not present end up being overlooked when they are not actively present. For those instructors who are detail minded they can create a spreadsheet and track the progress of their students. Some learning management systems provide analytics that allow an instructor to check on the progress of students in the course. The purpose of doing this is to pay attention to your students and how they are progressing.

How to Prompt Student Engagement

To assist educators with the process of prompting students' engagement in class I have developed a model called **ENGAGE**.

Examine class conditions as it can be conducive to or discourage active involvement. For example, do you post announcements that include a preview or wrap-up of the subjects or concepts for the week? Do you provide additional resources? Do you provide several methods of contact so that students can easily reach you? All of these strategies can help to create conditions that are conducive to learning.

Notice students' involvement and pay attention to their activities. If you wait until you provide feedback to determine who is active and who isn't, that may be too late to intervene. If there are features built into the learning management system that allow you to track students and their access to the course, this can help you identify students who are disengaging. You can also check who has completed the learning activities by the due date and develop a list of students who are past due.

Gauge the expected level of activity for an average student to establish a standard. As an instructor you develop a feel for the online class over time. You have a general idea of how much activity in the online class is indicative of an actively engaged student. Take that knowledge to help you develop a basic model and checklist that you can use, either mentally or in written form, to help monitor how your students are progressing.

Assess students and look for visual cues as you monitor their progress. As you monitor the progress of your students, and you consider how active they are based upon your expectations of their involvement, also consider how well they are performing. For example, a student can check in with the class on occasion by posting a brief discussion response and still not be substantively involved. A student who seems to be just getting by is someone who requires your time and attention.

Gain students' attention through some form of communication such as an email or a phone call if it appears they are not present or if they are disengaging from the class. It is important with an online class that you are proactively contacting your students any time you notice that they are struggling, not performing well, or they are not posting substantive contributions to the class discussions.

If you have developed a positive working relationship with your students, they may likely respond when you contact them by email. If you haven't been able to establish that connection, a phone call could be a helpful approach to reach out and establish your willingness to assist them. One of the primary challenges for making phone calls is finding a time that both the instructor and their students are available, especially if they are in different time zones.

Engage in the class as students will follow your lead. As a faculty reviewer, I have observed many online classes with students who were not actively engaged and it was a reflection of the level of engagement of their instructors. Students often develop a perception that their instructor doesn't seem to care about the class if they do not appear to be actively present. However, even if an instructor is highly visible and engaged it doesn't guarantee that students will also respond with that same level of involvement. What an active presence does is to encourage them to be engaged and involved.

Always Be Engaged in Your Class

For instructors, being highly engaged in an online class requires proactive effort and involvement. It is possible to catch struggling students before they are disengaged; however, it can be challenging because keeping track of students does take time. If you are allocating only enough time to complete the required facilitation tasks, you may find that isn't adequate for taking time to contact students and conduct outreach.

One of the first steps you can take is to develop a standard of acceptable engagement for an average student. By developing this standard, you can observe patterns and reach out to your students as needed. Overall, it is necessary to establish a plan for conscious awareness of your students if you want to keep them involved. Student engagement in an online class is related to their involvement in the learning process, their retention in a degree program, and it is a contributing factor to their overall success.

How to Diagnose the Needs of Your Students

The two most common reasons that a person will see a doctor is that there is an immediate health concern to be addressed or a routine checkup is needed for preventative maintenance purposes. A doctor will generally not have any preconceived ideas of what that patient needs unless there is an established history of care and treatment for that particular patient.

By listening to the patient and conducting an examination, the doctor looks for symptoms and/or makes an assessment of the patient's current condition as compared to a normalized standard. From that point a diagnosis is made and next steps are taken as needed. The most important aspect of this type of care is the relationship established between the doctor and the patient, and the patient's trust that the doctor will know how to address his or her needs.

Now consider an instructor, either one who teaches in a traditional classroom or one who teaches online. Do students view their instructors in a similar advocacy role? More importantly, what perception do students have about the role of an instructor?

For a traditional classroom, students evaluate their instructors based upon how they perform in the classroom, along with their disposition and mood, their availability to provide assistance when contacted, and a genuine concern (or lack thereof) for their developmental needs.

For online classes, students have to rely upon visual cues in the form of written messages and the implied meaning of those words. This includes what the instructor posts or states in written communication, along with the feedback provided. From my experience, most students contact their instructors when there an academic related concern. What can make teaching more effective is viewing instruction as a form of advocacy and proactively diagnosing each student and their academic or developmental needs.

An Instructor's Viewpoint

The majority of my experience in higher education has been in the field of distance learning and includes online faculty development. What I have found is that most instructors can manage the basics of their class in an effective and adequate manner, which means that questions are promptly addressed, discussion posts are completed as required, and feedback is provided within the required timeline.

However, managing an online class in an adequate manner does not always lend itself to creating the most dynamic and engaging classroom learning environment. The reason why is that students who are submitting their work on time, making an average grade, and never asking for assistance - they can be overlooked as students with the greatest needs often take a majority of the instructor's time.

When instructors are not able to see their students as they would in a traditional classroom, they usually reply upon the quality of posts and messages, along with the written assignments submitted, and that is how perceptual images are developed about each student. The challenge for relying on perceptions that are based upon written words is that it may not give a true or accurate reflection of each student as effort, frustration, and hard work cannot be seen.

It is only when students make an attempt to contact their instructors that any underlying issues or concerns become known, and the challenge is that students may not ask for assistance until an issue has escalated. That puts the instructor at a disadvantage as there are likely strong emotions involved and the lack of face-to-face interactions works against resolution of any issues, unless an instructor has been proactively working with students and has already established a productive relationship with them.

How to Diagnose Your Students

Taking an advocacy role means that as an educator you are being proactive in your approach to working with students. This involves taking time to get to know your students, interacting with them in a productive manner, learning about their academic needs, and assessing their capacity for ongoing development - regardless of the length of the class or the demands of classroom management.

If an instructor is concerned primarily with classroom conditions, meeting contractual requirements, and addressing students only when there is an issue, it is a reactive approach to instruction. For example, if an instructor is proactively working with students and a poorly developed paper is received, it is possible that the instructor will already know about the underlying reason and why the student is struggling. If the instructor has not established a relationship with the student there may be an assumption made the student is unable to write well or doesn't care about their progress.

Students that demand the most attention are the ones who are continuing to struggle or they are problem students who are challenging to work. Yet every student has developmental needs and a capacity for growth and that is why teaching, especially online teaching, is relational in nature.

Students cannot be accurately evaluated just by visual cues. For example, some students perform in an average manner and neither struggle or excel. Those students may perform in that manner because an instructor never took the time to work with them and learn about what they are capable of doing. There are diagnostic tools provided below that any instructor can implement as part of their instructional practice to learn about students and establish their role as that of advocate who conducts routine check-ups and assessments to resolve any academic concerns.

Pre-Assessments:

This could be a very useful tool at the start of a class and one that is designed to assess what the students know about the course topics, along with providing a current status of their writing skills. I realize that many online courses are pre-developed for instructors and offer little flexibility. This type of assessment could be non-graded and submitted to the instructor by email, which then provides an opportunity to begin working with students one-on-one and learning something about them.

Short Quizzes:

In traditional college classes there are generally quizzes and exams; however, in online classes those assessments are usually not implemented. I have found that a short quiz is a useful diagnostic tool as it tests the comprehension level of students for the course topics. It can be implemented after each unit, lesson, or module as a means of evaluating what was learned from the reading and other instructional methods used. This also allows an instructor to adapt their instructional practice as needed if there are topics that students are struggling with or do not understand.

Interim Short Assignments:

A short written assignment is also a helpful diagnostic tool, provided that it is given prior to the much larger or more significant written assignment, and there is time to provide feedback before the next assignment due date. That allows an instructor to assess how the student is progressing with the application of the concepts they have learned about, along with their progress with academic writing and formatting, as a means of helping them so they do well on the next paper.

With many online schools I have taught for there is a large assignment due at the end of the week and instructors are given seven days to provide feedback. Students have usually begun working on, and often submitted, the next assignment before feedback has been received. A short interim assignment can help to resolve that challenge for students and instructors.

Course Projects:

An instructor could implement the use of portfolio work, a personal or group wiki, or other projects that students must work on throughout the entire course, as a means of monitoring their progress and providing coaching, feedback, insight, and assistance as they complete project milestones.

Even the use of a mind map could be helpful as a means of assessing how the students are connecting concepts or topics they are learning about. If an instructor wants to test a student's critical thinking skills, an application written assignment can be given that requires students to resolve a problem or issue. All of these projects types provide an opportunity for the instructor to assess and work with their students.

Personal Attention and Instruction:

I've found that sending a check-in message to all students, not just those who are struggling, is an effective method of encouraging students to ask questions and work with me. An email could be sent at scheduled intervals throughout the course and then follow-up made for students who do not respond. I've also offered one-on-one appointments for any student who would like to discuss their progress or the course topics.

In addition, being available, accessible, and responsive is extremely helpful for establishing productive working relationships with students. If an instructor develops an "open door" type of policy, it helps students become comfortable asking questions, especially when they feel frustrated or uncertain.

I realize that the diagnostic tools provided only add to the amount of time required for class facilitation, and many instructors are working as adjuncts with limited time and availability. I've been in that role as well and understand how challenging it can be to keep up with a large class and many contractual facilitation requirements.

However, I also have been a student in a traditional and online class and the best memories I have are the ones that involved an instructor who took time to get to know me and work with me. A little extra attention was all I needed at times to feel re-energized and focused on my academic goals. That's the type of instructor I continue to aspire to be, one who is proactively diagnosing students and their needs, and ready to assess and address any concerns or issues that students may have during the class. I challenge you to be an advocate as well for you students. You will likely find that it is highly rewarding, for both you and your students.

End of Chapter Check-In

What Have You Learned?

What Are Your Strengths?

What Are Your Developmental Areas?

What Will You Apply to Your Teaching Practice?

CHAPTER 7.
ONLINE TEACHING CHALLENGES

Be Prepared for
the Unique Challenges of Online Teaching

Online teaching seems to be an appealing option for instructors, especially those who have not taught in this environment, because of the perception of convenience and the availability of jobs when compared to jobs for traditional colleges and universities - even though the number of online teaching jobs has declined over the past few years. It may also seem that an online class is easier to teach when it has already been fully developed.

What instructors quickly discover is that this is a unique learning environment and it can either be flat and one-dimensional with minimal interactivity or it has the potential to become two-dimensional in nature and highly interactive. A technologically-enabled, virtual classroom can be challenging for any instructor, unless they are prepared and willing to devote the time required to learn and adapt to this environment.

Challenge of Adapting to Technology

The online classroom is open at almost any time of the day or night and students are rarely present all at once, unless there is a scheduled mandatory online session. Students have to learn to adapt quickly and find the required information and resources. Some feel comfortable in a virtual environment and others will continue to struggle - either because they lack the skills or the classroom platform is not user friendly.

Whether students are limited or highly advanced in their computer literacy skills, they still must learn how to communicate and interact effectively when they are in class. If a student finds they are unable to function in this setting, or they become discouraged after making an unsuccessful attempt, their instructor may not know about it until that student is disengaged from the class or has completely withdrawn.

Students aren't the only ones who may find the online classroom challenging. Instructors are also likely to experience the same technological challenges, depending upon how comfortable they are with the use of technology and their level of computer literacy. For anyone who is interested in online teaching they must have a mindset that is open to learning and a willingness to continually improve their skills.

The effectiveness of online teaching depends upon instructors being able to engage their students through the use of virtual interactions and written communication.

Challenge of Teaching or Facilitating

A traditional college instructor has a fairly well-defined role. The classroom is structured so that the instructor is front and center, visibly present and responsible for guiding the learning process. There is a very clear chain of command and structure to this learning environment, and it hasn't changed much over time. This form of teaching is very similar to teaching in primary schools with a teacher-led approach and students acting as passive participants in the learning process.

In contrast, the online classroom has changed that structure simply because students and instructors are not always present at the same time, and instructors aren't at the front of the class dictating how the learning process should flow. This learning environment lends itself to a student-led approach as students can be more actively involved in the process. Many online schools call their instructors facilitators, believing that they are now facilitating a process rather than teaching. Regardless of the title given, the question is what do you want your role to be?

The answer depends upon your preferred teaching method. If you approach your instructional duties as a facilitator that may meet the contractual requirements. If you view your role as a teacher instead, this approach can create a different type of mindset and one that is more aligned with being an educator.

A teacher is someone who engages their students, is concerned with their ongoing academic development, and provides meaningful feedback. This is not to imply that a facilitator will not take a similar approach; however, facilitation implies overseeing and teaching emphasizes interactivity.

Challenge: Learning the Course Content

Online instructors are typically hired because of their background and experience, which is then matched to specific course subjects. If you are a subject matter expert for a particular class, you can add value to the learning process when you provide context for the course concepts - along with the inclusion of current issues and relevant scenarios. It is also likely that as an instructor you may not be a subject matter expert for all course topics and this is especially true if you are new to the subject being taught.

In a traditional college classroom instructors have to know the subject matter well as they often present a lecture about the course topics. What I've found with online instructors is that while they may be well-versed in certain businesses or industries they aren't always knowledgeable about all of the course subjects.

With an emphasis on facilitation instead of teaching, many instructors will facilitate the class by focusing on the required tasks instead of the content. This creates a missed learning opportunity as subject matter knowledge is an essential element of instructional posts and feedback.

My recommendation to instructors, especially those who are not familiar with all of the course topics, is to become an active researcher and obtain current resources that can be used during class discussions. You will also find that through the development of a solid base of research you will also be able to provide adequate and meaningful feedback for assignments. You will understand what students have written about in their papers and more importantly, have a point of reference to engage them further in the topics.

Challenge: Establishing a Virtual Presence

A teacher who is present and engaged in the class on a regular basis will connect with students and develop strong working relationships more easily than someone who is just logging into the classroom when required. It is all about the mindset held with regards to connecting with, working with, and getting to know students and their needs, strengths, and areas of development. This approach can be quite challenging for an online class.

It seems that there are two common mindsets among online instructors. One is to provide the required instruction and additional outreach or assistance only for those students who are struggling or contact their instructors. The other is to maintain some form of ongoing contact and support for students - through classroom posts, contact emails, feedback that asks questions, and other methods. A virtual presence is about paying attention to classroom conditions and all students. An instructor should never assume that students who are performing well or never contacting them are not in need of support or guidance. A virtual presence provides that support and it effectively creates social connections.

Students who "see" instructors present on a frequent basis begin to perceive that they are able to rely upon them to be available when needed. When students develop that type of perception they also become more responsive to feedback, they become better engaged in discussions, and they often mimic their instructor's level of involvement in the class.

Other Challenges: Time and Stress

One of the most important skills needed as an online instructor is the ability to manage your time. Whether you teach part-time or full-time there are many requirements that you must be prepared for each week and it includes the time needed to look for resources, participate in class discussions, and provide feedback, along with classroom management tasks. Often requirements such as the frequency of posting in the discussion threads and due dates for the feedback are defined in the faculty contract.

If you are an adjunct teaching more than one class and have other career related responsibilities, it is important to estimate how much time you have available to meet these requirements. The amount of time required for facilitation tasks each week depends upon the instructional approach you plan to implement. If you only want to meet the minimum requirements a lot less time will be needed than taking time to develop conditions that promote a highly engaging class.

Along with time management is a need to manage the potential for stress, which can happen at any point during a class. If you are hurrying to meet deadlines on a regular basis and feeling frustrated, the side effects of stress will likely show up in your class facilitation. Students are very aware of the tone of your messages based upon what they perceive while reading your discussion posts and email replies. If your time is not productively managed and the outcome or result is stress, you will likely start reacting to class conditions in a negative manner.

Overall, it is better to be organized and proactive in your approach to teaching online classes so that you can effectively and efficiently manage your workload - along with the potential for stress.

Develop Connections Even When Challenged

With a traditional college class, there is an opportunity to meet with students on a scheduled time and an instructor can visually assess their students, along with class conditions. It is very easy to tell when students are interested and when they are bored or tuned out. With an online class an instructor has to rely upon written cues instead of visual cues and be able to find a way to make this setting interesting and engaging.

Online teaching still involves the same level of commitment and dedication on the part of the instructor as teaching in a traditional classroom. The process of learning hasn't changed because of technology but the setting has and this creates new and unique challenges that educators must learn to adapt to. Once you have acclimated to this format of teaching, through time and practice, you will likely find that if you are proactively prepared for your tasks these challenges are not insurmountable and in time this can become a rewarding experience.

What to Do When Online Teaching Becomes Challenging

Educators and students alike know the challenges that distance learning can present. From potential technology issues to the challenge of time management, they both must learn to meet the basic requirements of a fast-paced course.

Online instructors have additional roles and responsibilities than can be both enjoyable and challenging. For example, in any online class there are going to be students with a wide variety of learning styles, needs, and interests - and knowing how to engage a diverse group such as this can be difficult even for the most experienced educators.

There are additional challenges that make the process of online teaching even more demanding. This includes addressing uncooperative students, students who don't seem to review their feedback and are unreceptive to constructive criticism, and students who fail to communicate in a respectful tone.

These are the types of issues that demand extra time and attention, and often lead to feelings of frustration on the part of the instructor. There are strategies that can be implemented when situations like these arise, especially when the issues involve more time and consideration than your typical instructional duties.

An Online Instructor's Workload

A majority of online classes are taught by adjunct instructors. That means those instructors who are teaching most of these classes are maintaining other responsibilities, just like their students. And similar to their students, they have a specific amount of time devoted for involvement in their classes. When they are online and working there are tasks that must be accomplished, usually with specific deadlines.

Every instructor hopes that students will be highly motivated, fully present when they are in class, and have a mindset that is open for learning. But as instructors know, it isn't always that way. Whenever a student issue does arise it can take up valuable time and cause some other duties to be pushed back.

What can save time is the development of a proactive plan for completing the required duties and establishing productive work habits. However, even with the best plans in place some students can be unpredictable and that is when an instructor and their facilitation methods are challenged.

The Online Student's Perspective

Students usually begin their classes from a positive perspective because it represents a fresh start. They hope that their new class is interesting and their new instructor either teaches in the same manner as the instructor for their last class or is completely different - if their outcome was not what they had hoped to receive or expected. This underscores the reason why challenges arise; students have an expectation about their involvement in the learning process and believe that instructors must conform to it.

As students work on the required tasks they utilize the same work habits from the last class and continue to perform in their most current pattern of productivity until there is a reason or need to change. If students are open to feedback and constructive criticism, they may be open to changing their approach to formulating posts and writing papers as a means of self-improvement.

However, for those students who hold a belief that they know best how to perform, they are likely to feel challenged by feedback received from their instructors. How students respond also determines their involvement in class as it progresses, and they always have a choice - maintain appropriate control of their classroom behavior or become uncooperative.

How Online Classes Become Challenging

Online classes are inherently challenging for instructors because there is no visual and verbal connection. They must maintain a highly engaged presence if they are able to keep the class on track. As part of maintaining that instructional presence instructors have to develop substantive discussion responses, be responsive to student questions, and develop feedback that supports students' progress and developmental needs.

Those responsibilities are the same for every class and over time instructors learn how to manage them in an effective manner. But student issues are the challenges that become more difficult to address and resolve.

There was a time when a non-responsive student was my biggest challenge as an online educator. Now I find there are students who have no problem expressing their feelings in an unprofessional manner. I'm still surprised when that happens because I reflect upon the time when I was an online student and I could not imagine speaking to an instructor in an unprofessional manner.

It can be easy for a student to hide behind anonymity, believing they are free to say whatever they like since they are not physically present. It seems to be a growing trend among students - those who do not have a filter with their communication and become aggressive, hostile, uncooperative, and defensive.

Strategies to Use When You Are Challenged

I've implemented the following strategies when challenged by online students and you may find them useful as well.

#1. Unresponsive Students:

If you are paying attention to your class and monitoring students' progress, you know when to intervene if you observe a student who has gotten off track. You hope that with supportive outreach attempts you can get them back on the right course. But if they don't respond, what do you do? The answer is to not give up and encourage them to contact to you through every option that you will allow or have established, including a phone call.

#2. Uncooperative Students:

This is the student who will not comply with any request you've made. It doesn't matter how small or significant the request was, you had a reason for making it. If the student is uncooperative the best approach is to send a message to them and ask for a reply. In addition, ask for contact and express your interest in their development and progress in class. The purpose is to neutralize any emotions that may arise by you or your students.

#3. Disengaged Students:

This is the student who is falling off the radar, who is not showing up for discussions, and/or may not be completing their assignments. The best approach for this type of student is to maintain outreach contact attempts until they respond in some manner. The purpose of these outreach attempts is to show them that they are valued and you want to assist them.

#4. Closed-Minded Students:

This is the student who does not see the need to change and will not read or utilize the feedback provided in any form. One approach that you can take is to be very specific in the feedback provided and never change in your approach to using that method of feedback. Within that feedback you can ask questions and encourage a dialogue with them. Try to establish a connection so that they eventually come to realize that the feedback provided is personalized and meant to help them.

#5. Students with Unprofessional Communication:

This is the student who cannot interact with you without resorting to communication that is unproductive. It may involve a long string of back-and-forth emails as the student tries to win their point of view. What to do in this situation begins with a response that demonstrates a caring attitude and willingness to assist them. Offer a phone conversation so that a connection can be made without the use of email. If they refuse to contact you and continue with their inappropriate communication, remind them of the student code of conduct. You should also follow any protocol in place for contacting other individuals at your school as needed.

Maintaining Standards of Excellence

This is the most important aspect of online teaching - instructors who maintain excellence in their style of facilitation, their interactions with students, and their expectations of students. As an instructor you can hold an expectation that students will provide substantive work, be willing to learn, and also meet the standards that have been established by the school.

To accomplish this goal, you must do more than facilitate a class and check off each requirement, you must also be open to creating conditions that are conducive to learning. And just as you expect of your students, you must be willing to receive constructive feedback and adapt your instructional methods as needed. When you have students who are challenging, even when you have done your best to create optimal class conditions, you must be prepared to address it quickly and in a receptive manner.

A challenging student is an indicator of a connection that was never fully established or has now been disrupted. And it doesn't matter that you have put in extra effort before with them or the class, you must do so now even more than ever. Every action you take must be done with the intent of establishing a new or renewed connection. This is not about what students will state on their end-of-course evaluations, it is about reaching out and getting through to a student who is stuck, withdrawn, or unable to be involved in the learning process with an open mind.

It is up to you to demonstrate your willingness to support their progress. Will it always work? Probably not; however, if you have done your part and offered to assist them you will either see a gradual change or they will remain stuck and continue to struggle. No matter what, never give up your coaching attempts - even with the most challenging students.

Poor Student Writing: What Is an Instructor to Do?

There is no question that every student, including undergraduate and graduate students, must learn to write well and often within a short period of time. Through my work as a faculty development specialist I've found that some instructors will diligently pay attention to the development of their students' academic skills, while others see it as too much work - passing students along without offering very much guidance.

I understand both perspectives to some degree as it may seem that students are not reading the feedback and guidance provided at times and if they are, they may or may not be making an attempt to improve how they write. For those instructors who make an effort to guide students and enforce academic writing standards, it may begin to feel as if the instructor is having to coerce those students who are not making progress.

Through my own experience with college-level teaching, especially as an online educator, I've found that all students have a capacity to learn and improve upon their writing skills. Most students will make an effort and eventually develop basic academic writing skills, some more quickly than others.

However, as any instructor knows it is always possible to have students in their class who do not make an attempt to address their poor writing skills and when the instructor intervenes, they may react in a negative manner. They may believe that their instructor is being mean or picking on them, and then the situation can escalate. Some institutions support their instructors and others ask the instructors to back down to avoid conflict and/or possible withdrawal.

If learning to write is such a challenge for students, what is an instructor to do?

Common Writing Errors

As students learn to develop their writing skills one of their first challenges involves learning how to convey their thoughts clearly and concisely, and in a manner that anyone who reads what they have written will be able to understand the meaning of their writing.

With entry-point classes, instructors often have to decipher and interpret what students have written. As I assess the writing of new students I'm asking myself the following questions: Are they writing "off the cuff" without investing much time and effort? Are they writing a research report and only stating what they have read? Are they sharing beliefs and opinions that may or may not be accurate? Or are they demonstrating what they have learned?

Some of the most common writing errors, beyond the basics such as grammar and spelling, includes making generalizations and assumptions, being reactive and writing an emotional response to the topic, or utilizing sources that are not suitable for academic work - such as online wikis and dictionaries.

Challenges for Students

Students are rarely given a pass if they continue to make the same mistakes, unless the instructor is willing to overlook their errors or told to go easy with the feedback provided to them. The reality is that instructors cannot and should not ignore poor writing, especially when it involves fundamental academic writing skills. This is extremely important for online students as they are communicating through the use of written words rather than verbal communication.

Students are challenged to learn to write quickly, correctly, and accurately. New students may first have to adjust their expectations as the reality of what it means to complete college-level, which means that unrealistic expectations or a negative attitude can get in the way of their progress. For some students, learning that they must improve their writing skills creates a line in the sand - and they decide to accept the responsibility or resist and create what may eventually feel like a coercive situation.

Instructors and Accountability

As a general rule, instructors are held accountable for the progress of their students, which means they cannot overlook mistakes and ongoing errors. Students often don't consider the instructor's perspective and that they are evaluated by the guidance provided and attempt to help students develop the necessary skills. If students move onto the next class and they continue to demonstrate poor writing the next instructor is either going to believe the prior instructor wasn't following the required standards, the students weren't making an effort, or both.

The challenge for instructors, especially those who are teaching online, is often having a short period of time to work with students and those who resist coaching or continue to make the same mistakes can be difficult to address and turnaround. It becomes even more challenging for instructors if they do not have institutional support.

I've seen many online courses be revised multiple times in an attempt to not only improve retention but to also ensure that more students are able to pass the class, even if they cannot write at the most basic or fundamental level. The revisions usually mean there are less writing assignments or fewer activities that require academic writing.

An Instructor Can Teach Focus

Student development is the responsibility of every instructor. It may not be possible to change the progress of every student who is struggling; however, it is possible to be proactive and offer guidance. Providing students with resources is the first helpful step. There are many free online writing resources that students and instructors alike can use.

Another helpful strategy is to take the time necessary to develop meaningful feedback that is viewed as supportive, while acknowledging the effort and progress made by students. A caring attitude on the part of an instructor may help to transform the reactive and negative responses of some students into that of a responsive and receptive mindset.

Not every student is going to be willing to change and if the instructor demonstrates responsiveness to those students who are trying, while never giving up their willingness to assist them, that will go a long way towards helping students learn and make gradual but steady improvements.

Every instructor develops a generalized feel for student writing over time, which means they know what constitutes strong writing and is able to easily identify indicators of poor writing. If there are numerous mistakes involving spelling and grammar, it can be easy to focus on trying to develop those aspects of writing while overlooking the bigger developmental issue - writing clearly and concisely.

I recommend that instructors teach students the power of focus by taking a subject or topic and working through it. I've developed a process for students to follow.

The following is my breakdown of the acronym **FOCUS**.

Find a position regarding the topic after completing the assigned reading.

Obtain credible, academic and scholarly research to substantiate a position.

Conduct a critical evaluation of the position, weighing both sides of the position and developing an analysis.

Update the position statement and create an engaging introduction to the paper.

State the final position as part of the well-informed and well-researched body of the paper, and develop a strong wrap up or overall summary for the conclusion.

I have found that the power of focus can help transform how students view the development of their writing skills. While they may still feel a sense of coercion because they are being forced to learn to write well, a supportive approach helps them realize their capacity for learning.

If instructors can help students develop their academic work from the perspective of learning to focus on the topic and developing a position statement, it will help them learn to write with clarity and purpose. Then as they begin to write more clearly and concisely, they will likely begin to care more about what they write and how they write it - including the seemingly minor details such as sentence structuring.

Student development is not always going to be an easy process for instructors but if there is a willingness to view it as a collaborative effort the outcome will likely be much better than creating an adversarial relationship. You cannot change all students or those who do not want to change, but you can make an effort to shift their thinking and ability to focus on learning and development.

Academic Honesty and Plagiarism

Academic honesty is an important topic for the field of online education. It is also as aspect of online teaching that is very challenging to uphold and instructors will either take the time to monitor student papers for originality or trust students to complete their work and comply with school policies.

While the increase in Internet accessibility has fueled the growth of online classes it has also made information much more readily available for student through a simple search engine query.

When students are developing discussion responses and written assignments they often look for sources to inform their work, especially when the topic is new to them. Students, especially newer students, often believe that they can "borrow" information without having to acknowledge the use of that information in any manner.

What instructors are finding on a regular basis are incidents of plagiarism, along with other forms of academic dishonesty. It is expected that online educators will uphold academic standards so it is important to understand the many types of violations that are possible, and proactively teach students how to produce original work.

Plagiarism: Accidental, Intentional

The most common form of academic dishonesty is plagiarism, which occurs when a student utilizes a source without providing a proper citation or acknowledging the words that have been used from that source. Most online schools have an originality checker or service available for instructors to use. If this service isn't available for an instructor it becomes imperative to spot-check sentences in each student's paper through an Internet search. Once an originality report has been received, or a manual review of the student's paper has been conducted, it is important to determine if the paper is entirely original.

If there are sentences or paragraphs that have been matched to existing sources, the next step to take is to make a distinction between accidental and intentional plagiarism. Accidental or unintentional plagiarism means that the student made an attempt of some kind to acknowledge sources used but forgot an element such as an in text-citation while still providing a reference list. Intentional plagiarism occurs when sources were clearly utilized and both an in-text citation and reference list were not provided.

An Instructor's Responsibility

It is imperative that online instructors utilize whatever resources are available to check the originality of student papers. Instructors develop a feel for their students' writing ability, especially through interactions within a discussion board, and one of the first signs of plagiarism occurs when the tone and/or word choice used in the paper is vastly different from typical discussion responses observed.

Another indicator that can be found within students' papers are different font sizes and colors, along with hyperlinks embedded in some of text. A plagiarism checker is the most effective tool because it will search a wide variety of Internet resources, including paper and essay mills. Most originality checking services maintain a repository of students' papers and provide an indication whenever a match to an existing paper was discovered.

What I have found interesting through my work as an online instructor with several for-profit schools is that there is often a standard put into place as to what percentage of a match within an originality report is acceptable.

For example, one school has a written policy that states 7% or less is acceptable when an instructor reviews an originality report. Another school has 13% as the maximum acceptable limit. The reason I find this interesting is that a student's paper should usually never have any match to existing sources if they have provided proper in-text citations and a reference list.

Reviewing the results of an originality report takes time and practice to accurately evaluate the results. It cannot and should not be assumed that just because there is a percentage listed in the report that plagiarism has occurred. Often the reference list in a student's paper is matched and can be quickly removed from the results. Then the rest of the paper can be evaluated.

Short phrases and anything considered to be common knowledge can usually be excluded, along with any sentences that have an in-text citation. If a sentence with a citation is highlighted there was usually an error made with formatting. Plagiarism occurs when there are sentences that have been directly copied and not acknowledged.

Other Forms of Academic Dishonesty

Another form of academic dishonesty is self-plagiarism and that occurs when a student has reused a paper from a previous class without first seeking their instructor's approval. Other types of academic dishonesty include copyright infringement, collusion, and cheating. Collusion and cheating occur when a student has asked someone else to help them complete their paper or they have done the work for them. This is harder to check in an online environment and an instructor cannot issue a sanction without definitive proof.

Academic Sanctions

When an incident of plagiarism has been detected an instructor must follow the guidelines that are in place. Typically, it is the role of the Academic Affairs department to make a final determination regarding the possibility of sanctions being taken.

Intentional plagiarism may result in a failing grade, a failed course, a written warning, and/or suspension from the school. It will usually be noted on the student's permanent record. Because of the serious nature of academic dishonesty, instructors must be proactive in their approach to monitoring originality and teaching students how to develop their own work while utilizing sources. It is only through this dual combination that academic standards will be upheld.

Of course asking instructors to take the time to monitor student papers, review originality reports and interpret them, and/or conduct an Internet search to check for originality takes time and makes the process of providing feedback much more complicated. This is especially challenging for adjunct instructors who have a fixed amount of time to complete the required tasks, which is the reason why many instructors I've worked with will conduct only a cursory review of student papers.

Another potential challenge is taking action on the part of an instructor as it could affect the overall GPA of a student and if they get upset with the outcome the situation may escalate. I've been told several times by those in administration to provide a warning in lieu of deducting any points to help prevent the student from dropping out of the class and/or their program. In other words, while there is a policy in place it may not be fully upheld as a matter of actual practice.

Regardless of how academic policies are upheld by a school, an instructor serves as the front line defense for prevention of academic dishonesty - especially plagiarism. While this is an aspect of online teaching that requires additional time and effort, it is essential for upholding academic standards and more importantly - teaching students how to develop written assignments that provide their own analysis, thoughts, and ideas rather than using existing sources to fill in their papers.

End of Chapter Check-In

What Have You Learned?

What Are Your Strengths?

What Are Your Developmental Areas?

What Will You Apply to Your Teaching Practice?

CHAPTER 8.
ONLINE TEACHING BEST PRACTICES

Fundamental Online Teaching Best Practices

Educators have discovered that online teaching can be exciting, rewarding, frustrating, demanding, and challenging all at the same time. The demands are often a direct result of requirements established by the school and the potential challenges are related to meeting the expectations in a satisfactory manner.

An online instructor's performance is measured according to the established contractual facilitation duties, end-of-course evaluations, and periodic classroom reviews. There is a minimum level of acceptable performance that is expected to be attained; however, meeting the minimum instructional expectations does not ensure that an instructor is effectively managing a class or creating optimal conditions that promote learning.

It is possible to become a highly effective and engaging online instructor by adopting common best practices that are student-focused. This occurs when an instructor feels comfortable working in a virtual class, has the time available to devote to their students, and becomes skilled in managing a class while coaching students towards meeting specific learning objectives.

Contractual Requirements

Most instructional basics are determined by a faculty contract, typically issued with each assigned class, along with other documents such as a faculty handbook. There are specific requirements for most instructional tasks, including the number of days an instructor is expected to check into the class, post participation messages, complete feedback, respond to student inquires and questions, and complete other similar tasks.

It is important to read and re-read the required school policies on a regular basis, in order to stay current with all of the expectations. It is also critical for your instructional practice to read all of the updates that are communicated to faculty, whether sent by email or posted within a faculty website, so there is never a surprise when changes or new processes are implemented.

Online Teaching Challenges

The initial challenge for new online instructors (and students as well) is making a transition from interacting with others face-to-face, with the benefit of visual and verbal cues, to digital communication. While some students may equate interactions on social networking websites with proficiency in communication through a technologically-enabled environment, there are some distinct differences.

One of those differences is related to communicating in complete sentences and articulating thoughts and ideas clearly and concisely, instead of relying on text speak or short, abbreviated statements. In addition, exchanges and messages shared through status updates or other online posts generally do not require the use of proper spelling and grammar. With time and practice any educator (or student) can become proficient with this form of communication. An instructor has the greatest responsibility to engage students and help them become acclimated to the virtual classroom.

Another perceived challenge for online instructors is the distance factor. A common misconception is that an instructor cannot help students if they cannot be seen. I've found through my own teaching practice that an online instructor has a potential for more interactions and involvement with their students if they take the time to nurture productive working relationships.

Essentials and Best Practices for Online Teaching

To meet the basic requirements, and address the potential online teaching challenges, there are strategies that every instructor needs for the development of their instructional practice if they are going to be a successful in their work as an online educator, and these essentials serve as best practices for online teaching.

#1. Supportive Instruction

An instructor's support is necessary to help promote a growth mindset in students, or one that involves a willingness to participate in the learning process and persist when challenges arise. Students need reassurance from their instructor as they work towards meeting the required objectives and develop the required academic skills. They have to learn to be productive and establish both habits and behaviors that allow them to succeed. The encouragement offered by an instructor can make a difference when students are faced with challenges. They will either persist and continue or quit and give up. Your support can also help to bridge the distance gap.

#2. A Positive Instructional Presence

The second essential requirement and best practice for online teaching is the establishment of a positive instructional presence. An instructor must be readily available and accessible for students based upon whatever methods are established and the time made available each week. For those instructors who are working as adjuncts, they will likely have other responsibilities to balance and an ability to log onto the classroom or check email may be limited during the day. However, it is possible to establish a working schedule and communicate the planned availability to students.

It is helpful for students to also know the general time frame planned for answering emails and questions, and when direct contact is available through office hours, chat, phone, or other options provided for them. An instructor's active presence is needed to assure students that they are in control of the class and aware of the conditions of this virtual environment. An instructor's involvement also has another effect, it is humanizing the learning experience for students and that will help them feel a sense of belonging to a community of real people rather than a collection of student identification numbers.

#3. Mastery of Your Academic Skills

The third essential requirement and best practice for all online educators is developing mastery of their own advanced academic skills. As a faculty peer reviewer I have observed poorly written and formatted discussion posts and student feedback, which does not necessarily interrupt the flow of the class; however, it creates a possible negative perception among students.

This is especially true for those students who are struggling with the development of their own academic skills and they observe numerous errors made by their instructor. If you are not confident with your writing skills or the required formatting style, seek out professional development workshops and classes. You could also find supplemental resources and for the materials you find that are helpful, share them with your students - I'm certain they will appreciate the additional assistance.

#4. Course Preparation and Ongoing Development

Another challenge related to time management is course preparation, which occurs if this is the first time a class is being taught or the first time an instructor teaches a class online. It is imperative that all materials are thoroughly reviewed as that information needs to be utilized as a knowledge base during class discussions, along with all learning activities and written assignments. It is possible that you may have subject matter expertise; however, it is necessary to become familiar with the materials that students are reading.

If you haven't read the materials the class discussions may not be as substantive as they have the potential to be and it may also be difficult to provide a thorough assessment of the written work submitted by your students if they have based their perspective on the assigned reading. Students look to what you post and what you state in your feedback to guide their comprehension and analysis of the course topics. If you aren't prepared it could result in a missed learning opportunity. Being informed and prepared means you are knowledgeable about the course topics and ready to guide the learning process.

#5. Cultivate a Love of Learning

Another essential requirement that is critical to an instructor's work with online teaching is cultivating a love of learning as a means of inspiring students. It would seem that this should be a natural characteristic of an educator; however, it can be easy to make this a lower priority when there are many other demands made, including facilitation responsibilities and tasks, along with classroom management.

One method of cultivating a lifelong learning approach is to have an intellectual curiosity about the subject you teach and conduct ongoing research to find sources that add to your knowledge-base and can be shared with your students. A love of learning may also inspire you to write and perhaps publish blog posts or articles related to your area of specialization and professional interests.

Whatever avenue you pursue, continue to be curious and find resources or associations that cause you to grow professionally. All of these options will allow you to increase and leverage your knowledge and expertise.

#6. Establish Expectations

Another basic instructional strategy best practice involves developing expectations for students, for both their perfor-mance and involvement in class. It is important to communicate what you expect, whether it is stated in the syllabus or a classroom post. Try to avoid holding your students accountable for something you believe they should do if it isn't obvious to them.

You can then provide clarity about the learning activities and assignments, taking into consideration specific elements that you want to emphasize. For example, if you are teaching an undergraduate class and students are just starting to learn a formatting style, clarify the expectations and provide a sample paper template or other resources that provide guidance. It is helpful to establish high expectations for your students, provided that it is attainable and you offer constructive feedback and support.

#7. Manage Your Time

An online instructor must manage their time efficiently and have a well-developed schedule in order to complete all of the required facilitation tasks on time. The two components of classroom facilitation that require the most time throughout the entire week includes participation in class discussions and providing meaningful feedback. If an instructor waits until the end of a class week to begin to work on the required instructional duties it can be easy to become overwhelmed and experience stress, along with potentially missed deadlines.

The unfortunate side effect of reaching this point is that it can show up in your attitude, the tone of your classroom posts, and the overall quality of your involvement, interactions, participation, and feedback - all in a potentially negative manner. Students will quickly pick up any hints of stress and frustration and this can cause them to disengage from the class.

#8. Be an Example for Your Students

The most important aspect of becoming prepared to teach online and excel as an online educator is to establish a high standard of excellence for your work and hold yourself accountable for the responsibilities that come with this position. Above all you must establish yourself as an example for your students, as someone who is fully engaged in the learning process, actively participating, concerned with academic integrity, always posting well-crafted messages and documents, and skillfully managing your classes.

You want to teach students the value of education and the powerful potential of distance learning through your interactions with them, the value you add to the class, and the manner in which you guide their development. The level of your involvement will influence how your students perform and respond to this virtual class environment. Follow these best practices as an important aspect of your instructional practice and you will establish a rewarding and meaningful career.

Develop Critical Online Teaching Strategies

The work of an online educator can be very demanding because of the nature of facilitating a learning process within a virtual environment when you cannot physically see or interact with your students. It can also be challenging for anyone who is working as an adjunct while balancing other career related responsibilities.

For those educators who have already taught online for some time they will likely have developed working habits that either assist them with meeting the contractual faculty requirements or cause them to miss important classroom deadlines and instructional functions. The level of an instructor's involvement in an online class can ultimately determine how much time and effort their students put into the class, which will in turn influence their performance.

Throughout my career as an educator I have taught countless online classes, reviewed hundreds of online classes as a faculty peer reviewer, and I have also trained hundreds of new online instructors as a faculty mentor. While most instructors can manage the general classroom management basics effectively, there are many other aspects of online facilitation that must be managed effectively to ensure that students are fully engaged in the virtual class, working to the best of their capabilities, actively participating in the discussions, and developing essential academic skills.

As a faculty peer reviewer there are common trends and issues I have observed that every instructor should be aware of as they consider what online teaching methods are effective and what areas of development may be needed.

What follows is another perspective regarding online teaching best practices and strategies that will help strengthen how you teach and interact with your students.

Online Teaching Standards

The standards that are established in an online classroom are often related to contractual requirements and specifies how the class should be managed. It is unlikely that a faculty contract could fully itemize every possible instructional strategy and technique that must be utilized to ensure a class functions properly or the instructor is performing to the very best of their ability.

What many online schools rely upon is the subject matter expertise of their instructors, ongoing classroom reviews, and the provision of faculty developmental resources. These standards are meant to ensure the class is run effectively but that is only a starting point for creating conditions that promote learning.

Common Habitual Patterns

The two most common habits that can either work for or against an instructor are habits of time and productivity. Instructors can develop the same issues that students do related to time management. For example, if an instructor's feedback is due within seven days and they wait until day five to begin they could run into a time crunch.

It is very easy to tell when an instructor has run out of time simply because it shows up in feedback that appears to have been hurriedly put together. Some instructors believe that students rarely (or never) read their feedback so the minimum effort possible should be enough. However, if that is an accurate perspective then the only way to change that perception about feedback is to begin making it meaningful.

Another common habit is what I refer to as instructional sameness and that simply refers to relying upon the same teaching style repeatedly without ever adding in any variety. This often applies to how an instructor interacts with students during class discussions. If an instructor has not put time and thought into their discussion question responses, then the conversations will not be as engaging as they could be.

For example, responding to students and complimenting them on their posts without asking thought-provoking questions could likely end that particular discussion. It is also important for an instructor to share their professional insight and additional resources to help further the students' understanding of the course topics.

Observations as a Peer Reviewer

As a peer reviewer it is fairly easy to look at a class and quickly ascertain the level of effectiveness of an instructor based upon the interactions that are present or missing in the class. When instructors become habitually late with their feedback or missing other requirements, and their productivity in the classroom is minimal, over time their performance will typically decline. Within a virtual environment, where a strong online presence is needed, students pick up on the involvement level (or lack thereof) of their instructors. It comes as no surprise that many students will also begin to disengage from the class if their instructor is not actively involved.

An issue that comes up on occasion is the tone that is used by the instructor in their digital communication. Everything that an instructor writes, which is in everything they post, has a perceived tone and that means all communication must be carefully thought out. If a student has challenged the instructor the best strategy is not to respond right away but to type out a response in another document and then edit it in a rational rather than emotional manner.

Another area of online teaching that I have observed and would recommend as a reminder to all instructors is to be responsive to students. When a student asks a question that is a time to make a true connection with them by assisting them with a genuine concern for their academic well-being. It is too easy to send out quick replies and then discourage students from ever contacting you again. Student relationships in an online classroom are even more important because of the lack of a physical presence, along with verbal and non-verbal cues.

Critical Online Teaching Strategies

An educator can implement any or all of the following strategies to improve their online teaching process, and in any order.

#1. Decide that You Want to Create an Engaging Environment

At present the number of opportunities for online educators is less than the pool of people who want to teach online classes. That means you must establish yourself as a distinguished educator rather than someone who just meets the minimum requirements if you want to continue to receive classes or new opportunities. But more importantly, if you are determined to create an environment that is conducive to learning then you need to make time available throughout your week to ensure that you are actively involved in your class and responsive to your students.

#2. Make a Commitment to Ongoing Professional Development

There is a correlation between instructors who lose effectiveness with their approach to teaching online classes and a lack of professional development. This does not mean you have to seek out another degree, unless it is part of your career plan. What you can do is to establish areas of professional interest and then conduct research. Most instructors have access to online library databases so it can be easy to find current research that will inform your teaching practice.

In addition, there are a number of professional journals you can read and associations you can join that are related to the field of adult education and online learning. Another method of gaining resources and connecting with other educators is to utilize social media such as Twitter, as you can gain connections to a global academic community.

#3. Use the Feedback You Have Been Provided

Just as you tell your students to read their feedback and ask questions, so too should any online instructor utilize feedback from peer reviews or other classroom audits. If those reviews are only conducted annually then take a look at the resources provided by your school, reacquaint yourself with the faculty standards that are in place, and conduct your own self-analysis or classroom audit. A formal faculty review of a class can provide you with a wealth of information if you are open to receiving constructive criticism. I understand that this type of feedback is never perfect and may seem to be subjective in nature; however, take from it what you can to improve how you teach online classes and it will be of benefit to you and your students.

#4. Establish Teaching Goals

The question that online instructors should always consider is whether they want to work towards average or exceptional performance. This means you either meet or exceed the required standards that are in place, along with your own personal standards of excellence. It is also important to consider if you are functioning in the classroom for yourself and with a focus on what you are doing, or you are concerned about the well-being of your students and what you can do to ensure their educational needs are met.

Instructors can either be present in the class only when they are required to be there or they can be frequently involved. They can also be reactive to conditions or proactively working to ensure that students are engaged in the process of learning and academic development. Every instructor has room to grow no matter how long they have been teaching online classes. The success of an online educator, and the success of their students as well, depends upon their willingness to learn, grow, and adapt their classroom facilitation skills.

Five Strategies Every Online Instructor Needs

There many people who want to make online teaching a career option either part-time or full-time - if they can find teaching opportunities. This has made finding new positions highly competitive. For those who are already teaching online, they want to make certain there are plenty of opportunities still made available to them. Once you are offered a course to teach you have to make a decision that you are going to be more than an average instructor if you are going to continue to receive future class offerings. You must also decide that you will devote the time necessary to create conditions that are conducive to the development and well-being of your students. It is not an easy task to manage an online class and excel as an educator, but there are strategies you can implement to meet these demands and allow you to be successful.

A Virtual Classroom

One of the first aspects of online teaching that you must learn to be comfortable with is the use of technology because everything that you do depends upon how well you can utilize the technological tools that are available. If you have only taught in a traditional classroom you will find it can be very challenging at first because you are no longer at the center of the learning experience. Over time it does become easier to navigate through the classroom and learn how to utilize all of the resources available. Some of the most common learning management systems (LMS) in use today by online schools include eCollege, Sakai, Blackboard, Moodle, and Canvas. To be successful in this type of classroom environment you have to be willing to use technology, be flexible in your instructional strategies, and ask for help whenever you need it.

Digital Communication

Another aspect of the online classroom that can take time to learn is the use of digital communication, especially since students are not always present at the same time. In a traditional classroom you have the ability to interact with students, provide direction and instructions, and offer clarification as soon as it is needed. Communicating in an online classroom is quite different and the content of what you post, including everything you write or post, can either connect students to this environment or discourage them and cause them to disengage.

The first thing that you must be concerned with is the mechanics of what you write as poorly worded and constructed posts or messages can create a negative impression of your work as an instructor. But most of all it is the perceived tone of your messages that can cause the most damage if what you write is not carefully constructed. For example, if you feel frustrated about a student or situation in your classroom and that is conveyed in what you write, a student or possibly the entire class, will begin to tune you out or no longer trust you care about their needs.

Being More Than Average

It is possible that anyone can step in and do the minimal amount of work necessary to successfully meet all of the facilitation requirements; however, you have to consider if that is enough to create conditions that are conducive to learning. What most online instructors find is that they have to be more than average if they want to be successful in this environment. All online instructors are subject to an annual review, at a very minimum, and they are measured according to the degree that they are involved in their classes and addressing students' questions and concerns.

If you want to continue teaching online classes, it will be worth your time to become more than an average instructor and stand out as one of the best. Of course as an adjunct there are never any guarantees about continued employment so you have to think of it as an investment in your career. If you are receiving outstanding performance reviews, and any type of rewards or recognition along the way, all of that can be listed on your resume.

You will also find it much more enjoyable when students are responding in a positive manner because of your performance and they are highly engaged in the class because they are modeling what you do.

Five Strategies You Can Use

There are five strategies that can be implemented at any time to strengthen your work as an online educator.

#1. Be Visible in Your Class

Students need to see that you are present in the class as it shows them from a perceptual viewpoint how dedicated you are to the class. This means they need to see you actively involved in the discussions, posting announcements when you have additional information or updates to share, and answering their questions quickly.

It is possible that you can follow the minimum guidelines put in place by your school, as to the number of days you must be present; however, if you want to manage class well you should plan on checking in with your class on a frequent basis.

#2. Be Engaged in Your Class

Becoming visible in your class is only the first step and the next building block in the process of creating a highly interactive class is to establish rapport with students. Students want to know they can connect with you on some level and have meaningful interactions either through class discussions or one-on-one communication. What do you think students will perceive if you are barely involved in the class and only provide hurried answers to their questions, or minimal responses to their discussion question posts? Keep in mind that online students can easily disengage and it takes a lot of work to bring them back once they have begun to disengage.

#3. Be Prepared for Your Duties

As an online instructor you must be ready to commit the time necessary to be highly involved in your class because of the required deadlines, the lengthy class discussions, and the necessity to be proactively involved in the development of your students. If you are just trying to get by you will find that over time some requirements begin to get backlogged and it will be reflected in the lack of progress by your students. Keep in mind that everything that you are doing in the online classroom as an instructor needs to be focused on the learning process and helping students experience a positive classroom or learning environment.

#4. Be Firm, But Fair

You will be expected to uphold the academic standards that are in place by your school and it can include everything from policies and procedures to academic honesty. You can take the position that you are going to be very strict and rigid in your application of these rules or you could be firm, fair, and understanding of your students' experience as they are trying to navigate their way through all of these requirements. For example, writing is likely to be a common challenge for your students and you can either demand their compliance or you can hold them to the required expectation and support their development by providing meaningful feedback and offering resources to assist them.

#5. Be Responsive

Your interactions with students must have a responsive tone if you are going to get them to respond to you and work with you. For example, if a student sends you an email and ask for assistance and the only response you give them is to check the course syllabus then they will likely not ask you again. But if you work with students to ascertain where it is they are struggling or what they are trying to understand you will demonstrate to them that you care about them as a student and this is what can go a long way towards keeping them engaged in the class. Your work as an online instructor is not just getting through the class; it is guiding students through the learning experience.

Exceptional Results

If you implement all of these strategies will every student earn an "A" grade for the class and give you positive feedback at the end of the class? Of course the answer is no but that is not the point of being highly visible, engaged, and responsive to your students. The goal of your involvement in the class is to provide them with an engaging environment to explore the course topics and guide them in the development of their academic skills. The more time that you invest into your classroom instruction the more that they will be personally transformed by the time that they have reached the end of the class.

Students will either have picked up tools they need to continue their developmental progress or they will have a greater understanding of the areas that need to be worked on. An online instructor is someone who is not just managing a class, they are involved in the process of educating adults. You can put in the minimal amount of time required and hope that students make it through the class, or you can become more than an average instructor and experience exceptional results both in your work as an educator and the outcomes of your students.

Insight from a Faculty Reviewer

The work of an online instructor can be very demanding because of the nature of facilitating a learning process within a virtual environment. It is also a challenge for someone who is working as an adjunct and has other career related responsibilities. For someone who has been doing this awhile they will likely have developed working habits that assist them in meeting the mandatory requirements. Some of these habits may be effective while other habits need further development.

Throughout my career as a faculty development specialist, I have reviewed hundreds of online classes and I have also trained new online instructors as a faculty mentor. While most instructors can manage the basics there are many other qualities that are necessary to ensure students are fully engaged, working at the best of their capabilities, and developing the required academic skills. There are common trends and issues I have observed that any instructor should be aware of and work to improve upon.

Online Teaching Standards

The standards that are established in an online classroom are often related to contractual requirements that involves how the class is managed. This can include deadlines for providing feedback, participation requirements, a timeline for answering questions, and other specifics related to how the course is set up and run. There has never been an instructional contract that fully itemizes every possible strategy and technique that must be utilized to ensure the class functions properly or that the instructor is performing to the best of their ability.

What many online schools rely upon is the expertise of their instructors, ongoing classroom reviews, and the provision of faculty developmental resources. These standards ensure the class is run effectively but that is only the starting point for schools to make certain that classroom conditions are conducive for learning and the instructors are working towards creating a positive learning experience.

Common Habitual Patterns

The two most common habits that can either work for or against an instructor are habits of time and productivity. Instructors can develop the same issues that students do as related to time management. For example, if an instructor's feedback is due within seven days and they wait until date five to begin reviewing papers they could run into a time crunch. It is very easy to tell when an instructor has run out of time simply because it shows up in feedback that appears to have been hurriedly put together. Some instructors believe that students never read their feedback so the minimum effort possible should be enough. However, if that is accurate then the only way to change a perception like that about feedback is to begin making it meaningful.

Another common habit is what I refer to as sameness, and that simply refers to using the same teaching style repeatedly without ever adding in any variety. This often applies to how an instructor interacts with students during class discussions.

If enough thought is not put into the responses developed by an instructor, the discussions are not going to be as engaging as they should be. Often that means instructors are not asking thought-provoking questions and sharing insight or additional resources within their responses.

Observations as a Faculty Reviewer

As a faculty reviewer it is easy to look at a class and quickly ascertain the level of effectiveness simply because of the number of classes I have observed. When instructors become habitually late with their feedback or missing other require-ments, and their productivity in the classroom is minimal, over time their overall performance will typically decline. Within a virtual environment, where a strong online presence is needed, students pick up on the frequency (or lack thereof) of the involvement of their instructors. It comes as no surprise that many students will begin to disengage from class if their instructor is not actively involved, or at a very minimum their performance may decline.

Another issue that comes up on occasion is the tone that is used by the instructor in their written communication. Everything that an instructor writes, along with everything they post, has a perceived tone and that means all communication must be carefully thought out. If a student has challenged the instructor in some manner, the best strategy is not to respond right away but to type out a response in another document and then edit it in a rational rather than emotional manner.

Another area of online teaching that I have observed and would recommend as a reminder to all instructors is to be responsive to students. When a student asks a question that is a time to make a true connection with them by assisting them with a genuine concern for their academic well-being. It is too easy to send out quick replies and then discourage students from contacting you again. Student relationships in an online classroom are even more important because of the lack of a physical presence, along with verbal and non-verbal cues.

Strategies for Self-Development

There are strategies that any online educator can use to develop their instructional practice, and these are strategies that I continue to use and implement.

#1. Decide that You Want to Create an Engaging Environment

At present the number of opportunities for online educators is less than the pool of people who want to teach online classes. That means you must establish yourself as a distinguished educator rather than someone who just meets the minimum requirements - if you want to continue to receive classes or new opportunities.

But more importantly, if you are determined to create an environment that is conducive to learning then you need to make time throughout your week to ensure that you are actively involved in your class and responsive to your students.

#2. Make a Commitment to Ongoing Professional Development

Often instructors who are losing effectiveness with their approach to teaching online classes is related to a lack of professional development. This does not mean you have to seek out another degree, unless that is part of your career plan. What you can do is to establish areas of professional interest and then conduct research.

Most instructors have access to online library databases so it is very easy to find current research that will inform your teaching practice. In addition, there are a number of professional journals you can read and associations you can join that are related to the field of adult education and online learning. Another method of gaining resources and connecting with other educators is to utilize social media, such as Twitter, as you can gain connections to a global academic community.

#3. Use the Feedback You Have Been Provided

Just as you tell your students to read their feedback and ask questions, so should any online instructor utilize feedback from class reviews or other classroom audits. If those reviews are only received annually then look at the resources provided by your school and determine what standards are in place so that you can conduct your own self-analysis.

An annual review of your work as an educator can provide you with a wealth of information if you are open to receiving constructive criticism. I understand that this type of feedback is never perfect and can be subjective in nature; however, take from it what you can to improve how you teach your classes and it will be of benefit to both you and your students.

Establish Teaching Goals

The question that any online instructor should ask themselves is whether they want to be average or exceptional. This means you either meet or exceed the standards that are in place, along with your own personal standards of excellence. It is also important to consider if you are functioning in the classroom for yourself and with a focus on what you are doing, or you are concerned about the well-being of your students and what you can do to ensure their educational needs are met.

An instructor can either be occasionally present in class or they can be highly involved. They can be reactive to conditions or proactively working to ensure that students are engaged in the process of academic development and knowledge acquisition. Every instructor has room to grow no matter how long they have been teaching online classes. Your success, and the success of your students, depends upon your willingness to learn, grow, and adapt your facilitation skills.

End of Chapter Check-In

What Have You Learned?

What Are Your Strengths?

What Are Your Developmental Areas?

What Will You Apply to Your Teaching Practice?

CHAPTER 9.
PROFESSIONAL DEVELOPMENT

Why Educators Need Professional Development

Professional development is an annual requirement for many schools and when it is required is usually stated as a specific number of hours that must be completed. Whether or not you work for a university that states this as a requirement for your position, professional development needs to be thought of as an ongoing process rather than a one-time event. When you are engaged in some form of professional learning, you are provided with an opportunity to develop and refine your instructional skills, acquire current and relevant knowledge, learn methods for becoming an effective educator, and acquire resources that help you create a meaningful learning environment.

Teaching a class is not just about showing up and giving students course materials and making certain that your facilitation requirements are met. Instead, learning is an interactive process with many vital components that are enhanced through your own self-reflection, addressed by adult learning theories, and are made meaningful as you make the transformation from being an instructor to an educator. While instructors may view this obligation as being time-consuming, if you consider this to be an opportunity for growth and you will quickly discover the benefits for your work as an educator.

Identify Your Own Areas of Need

Before you begin taking courses, signing up for webinars, or start researching available options for meeting this developmental requirement, take time for self-assessment. One of the most effective strategies you can use is that of self-reflection after a course has concluded. Use this time, even if it is a brief period before the next course begins, to consider what worked well in the prior course and what areas you would like to improve upon. This can include everything from your instructional practices to how you complete the required tasks and manage your time.

Through self-assessment, ask yourself about your strengths as an educator and challenges you have experienced. You can also ask yourself the following questions: Do you find class discussions are enjoyable and students respond to you, or do you find it challenging to engage students in the discussions? Is the feedback you've provided meaningful or do you view it as a task to complete quickly?

The approach you take can greatly impact your students and their progress. Are students learning and how do you know if they have learned? The more questions you ask immediately following the conclusion of a class the more likely you'll have accurate answers as relevant details can be forgotten over time.

Important Adult Learning Theories

The process of self-improvement also provides you with an opportunity to reflect on your knowledge of adult learning and what areas of research you may still need to explore. Some of the basic adult learning theories and concepts that can inform your work as an educator include andragogy, self-directed learning, transformational learning, motivation, engagement, and cognition. Andragogy is a theory about teaching adults that is in contrast to pedagogy, which is a theory about teaching children. According to the theory of andragogy, adults want to be actively involved in the learning process and they have both existing knowledge and experience that needs to be acknowledged. This is contrast to pedagogy, which holds that children must be taught how to learn and what to learn. Adults are also self-directed by nature and that means they want to be responsible for their involvement; however, that level of responsibility can vary from student to student.

Transformational learning refers to changes that are experienced by students as they participate in the class. As students are engaged in the learning process they become transformed. The use of critical thinking is a method of creating this type of transformative experience. Motivation refers to the amount of effort a student exerts and it can be influenced by internal and external factors, some of which are directly controlled by an instructor. Engagement refers to the level of involvement students put into their studies and it can be affected by such factors as emotions, feelings, and interactions with others. Cognitive processing refers to mental functioning that students use as they are involved in class, and higher cognition or cognitive processing can be prompted through critical thinking.

Other concepts to explore to inform your class facilitation include the process of knowledge creation, managing diversity, understanding the different types of learning styles, and the impact of learning disabilities on performance in the online class.

Transforming from Instructor to Educator

Instructors are often hired because they are subject matter experts in their particular field and/or they have experience in a relevant career field. However, possessing career knowledge and experience is not always enough to be an effective instructor. As a faculty trainer and reviewer I have examined many classes where the instructor was very knowledgeable about the subject they were discussing but they didn't fully understand the process of learning. Even though they were able to complete the minimal facilitation requirements their overall instructional approach was often ineffective.

Becoming an educator means that you can facilitate engaging class discussions, provide feedback that contributes to the academic progress of your students, and you are able to communicate and interact with students in a meaningful manner. Every aspect of an instructional practice needs to be done with a well-defined purpose.

Resources You Can Use

One of the first resources you can utilize are websites dedicated to adult learning and more specifically, online learning.

One example is MERLOT, which stands for Multimedia Educational Resource for Learning and Online Teaching. There is a page that offers links for faculty development you may find useful. Another organization is Sloan-C or the Sloan Consortium, which offers resources and the Online Learning Journal (formerly titled the Journal of Asynchronous Learning or JALN).

If your school has a Center for Teaching and Learning you may want to review what's available, especially if there are online webinars you can attend. Another helpful publication to look for is the Journal of Online Learning and Teaching (JOLT).

Finally, look for professional communities such as groups offered through LinkedIn that are specifically related to higher education and online teaching.

Ongoing Commitment to Learning

Finding and utilizing resources allows you to develop your instructional practice and it encourages you to become a lifelong learner, just as you want to encourage your students to become. Through ongoing development, you can become more than an instructor who manages the process of facilitation, you can transform to an educator who effectively promotes learning.

As an online educator it is especially important to be familiar with changes in technology, which allows you to present information through new methods and with different tools. It is important that you stay up to date and be current not only with technological tools but current thinking and practices in the field of online learning that you will find published through scholarly articles and other resources.

Through the process of self-development, you will provide yourself with an opportunity to experience professional growth in a manner that informs all aspects of your work. Consider what your students need and commit to viewing your instructional work as being adaptive and in need of continued development.

Your professional development should be ongoing, just like the process of learning, regardless of the length of time you have been an educator. The more you learn the more effective you will become with your instructional practice, allowing you to create a meaningful and purposeful learning experience for your students.

Strategies to Use for Professional Development

What is the essence of online teaching?

Should an online instructor be referred to as a teacher, facilitator, educator - or perhaps all three are applicable?

In my experience with online teaching, all three of those words apply as an online instructor must know how to teach a subject, facilitate a learning process, and be an educator by knowing how adults learn. At the heart of online teaching are the relationships and interactions developed and sustained with students, the personal connections made that humanize the learning experience, and the discussions that are nurtured to engage students in meaningful conversations.

The work of an online instructor can become very demanding because of the nature of facilitating a learning process within a virtual environment when instructors cannot physically see or interact with their students.

I've learned through my work in faculty development that most instructors can manage the basic general facilitation duties. However, there are many other aspects of online teaching that must be learned as a product of time and practice to ensure that students are fully engaged in the virtual class, working to the best of their capabilities, actively participating in the discussions, and developing the essential academic skills. In other words, online teaching is more than just a function - it is a process to be nurtured.

To become a productive, effective, and engaging instructor, a commitment must be made to ongoing self-reflection and development, along with personal and professional growth, if an instructor is to build a successful long-term career in the field of distance learning.

Establishing Standards for Teaching

There are two types of standards that an online instructor needs to consider as part of their ongoing development and the first is established by the school, which is typically stated as contractual facilitation duties. These duties outline specific responsibilities that must be met as a condition of continued employment. The responsibilities are often related to "what" the instructor is to teach and "when" specific tasks must be completed.

The expectations are stated in terms of classroom functions that may include a number of discussion posts, feedback deadlines, and the list continues. It is highly unlikely that a faculty contract can fully itemize every possible requirement as a means of ensuring the instructor is performing to the very best of their ability.

There are likely additional standards in place that are stated within a faculty handbook or outlined as faculty procedures that provide a quality measurement tool. What many schools rely upon is the use of classroom audits and reviews, along with the provision of faculty developmental resources when performance issues are identified.

The establishment of standards is meant to ensure that classes are facilitated effectively; however, that is only a starting point for creating conditions that promote learning. The other set of standards that are necessary are those that each instructor develops for their instructional practice. These are personal and professional standards that establishes the "how" for online teaching; how well an instructor performs what is required.

Developing New Routines

Over time every instructor develops routines as a means of managing their classes effectively and efficiently. There are common habits that can either work for or against an instructor and includes the habits of time and productivity. It is possible for instructors to develop the same issues that students do as related to time management. For example, if an instructor's feedback is due within seven days and they wait until day five to begin the review process it is possible to run into a time crunch.

It is easy to tell when an instructor has run out of time as it shows up in feedback that appears to have been hurriedly put together. Some instructors have a perception that students never read their feedback so the minimum effort possible is thought to be enough when it comes to developing the feedback. However, if that is accurate then the only way to change that perception about feedback is to begin to make it meaningful.

Another common habit is what I refer to as instructional sameness and that refers to relying upon the same teaching style over time without ever adding in any variety or creating new instructional strategies. This is related to how well an instructor interacts with students during the class discussions. If an instructor has not put time and thought into their discussion question responses, then the conversations will not be as engaging as they could be.

For example, responding to students and only complimenting them on their posts, without asking thought-provoking questions as a means of follow up, could likely bring that particular discussion to a halt. It is also important for an instructor to share their professional insight and experiences, along with additional resources to help further the students' understanding of the course topics.

Strategies to Use for Professional Development

There is a correlation between instructors who lose effectiveness with their approach to teaching online classes and a lack of professional development. This does not mean you have to seek out another degree, unless it is part of your career plan, but you can develop strategies that will prompt your growth and improve your instructional practice.

#1. Find Opportunities to Engage with Other Professionals

What will help to promote professional development is finding opportunities that allow you to engage in communities of professionals who share a similar interest in online teaching and distance learning, which will help you gain new perspectives and strategies that in will turn prompt your own self-analysis and assessment.

Start by looking at the associations related to the field of distance learning and review the resources offered. LinkedIn has numerous groups you can join and engage in discussions that are relevant to the field. You can also look for webinars or classes that your school offers as a means of engaging with other educators at your school.

#2. Develop Networking Opportunities

Another method of gaining resources and connecting with other educators is to utilize social media, such as Twitter or LinkedIn, as you can gain networking connections with a global academic community. As a result of my involvement in these types of groups I have been asked to contribute articles and blog posts, and participate in research studies. Typically, networking is viewed as a job search strategy and while that certainly applies, there is a greater purpose and that is to discover new instructional ideas and methods.

#3. Strengthen Your Knowledgebase

One of the first self-development practice you can begin to invest in is learning adult education basics. Look for authors on the LinkedIn Pulse Education Channel who publish relevant work. What you can also do is to establish areas of professional interest and conduct research.

Two helpful topics to read further about include andragogy and critical thinking. Most instructors have access to online library databases so it can be easy to find current research that will inform your teaching practice. For example, there are a number of professional journals you can read that are related to the field of adult education and online learning.

#4. Develop Your Subject Matter Expertise

As an instructor you must know your subject matter well and be able to teach it.

Most instructors are hired because of subject matter expertise, a specific number of credit hours gained that are related to the subject field, and/or related experience. Does that mean you need to know everything possible about that subject?

While you may hold varying degrees of knowledge it would be beneficial for your teaching practice and your classes to continue to read about current research in the field, new theories and ideas, and find new case studies or real world examples that add value to your class, especially during the class discussions.

#5. Utilize Self-Reflection as Learning

This is an area of self-development that can be challenging for instructors because of the time involved to sit uninterrupted and reflect upon their teaching practice. Most online instructors are busy and weekly duties don't stop until a class ends. But that is a time when valuable insight can be obtained, if an instructor will make an effort to take a few minutes and itemize what went well during the class, the teaching challenges that came up, and what was learned that can be applied to their overall instructional strategy. If everything went well and there were no challenges to your instructional practice, then you have confirmed that your teaching practice is effective.

#6. Experience Your Students' Perspective

What can be an eye-opening experience for online instructors is to enroll in an online professional development class and gain insight into what the student experience is like. You may decide by the end of that class that you already have an effective instructional practice now; however, you may also pick up some new tips and techniques. For example, I've learned about new technological tools that can help bring my instruction to life in a virtual class as a result of my involvement in professional development classes and webinars.

#7. Utilize Feedback You've Received

Just as you tell your students to read their feedback and ask questions, so too should any online instructor utilize feedback from class reviews or other classroom audits. If those reviews are only conducted annually then take a look at the resources provided by your school, reacquaint yourself with the faculty standards that are in place, and conduct your own self-analysis or classroom audits.

A formal faculty review of a class can provide you with a wealth of information if you are open to receiving constructive criticism. I understand that this type of feedback is never perfect and may seem to be subjective in nature; however, take from it what you can to improve upon how you teach online classes and it will be of benefit to both you and your students.

What Is Your Teaching Purpose?

At present the number of opportunities for online educators is less than the pool of people who want to teach online classes. That means you must establish yourself as a distinguished educator rather than someone who just meets the minimum requirements if you want to continue to receive classes or new opportunities.

More importantly, if you are determined to create an environment that is conducive to learning then you need to make time available throughout your week to ensure that you are actively involved in your class and responsive to your students. The question to consider is whether you want to work towards attaining average or exceptional performance. This means you either meet or exceed the required standards that are in place, along with your own personal standards of excellence.

It is also important to consider if you are functioning in the classroom for yourself and with a focus on completing the required tasks, or you are concerned about the well-being of your students and what you can do to ensure their educational needs are met. Instructors can either rely upon the same teaching methods that they have used for many classes or over several years, or they can engage in professional development as a means of helping their instructional practice to evolve and improve. Every instructor has room to grow professionally no matter how long they have been teaching online classes. The success of any online educator, as well as the success of their students, depends upon the willingness of the instructor to learn, grow, and adapt their classroom facilitation skills.

What Inspires You to Teach

You may remember how you got started as an instructor, but do you recall what inspires you to continue teaching? The instructional duties of an educator require advanced planning and well-defined time management skills, especially if you have multiple projects or responsibilities to balance. If you teach in a traditional classroom you have to plan for class that typically meets on a specific day of the week; and if you teach online, it is expected this you will be actively engaged in your class throughout the week.

What inspires you to devote the time necessary to create a meaningful learning experience, knowing that you will need to make a significant commitment of your time?

Yes, it is your responsibility to meet the requirements of your job, but what drives you to succeed? Is it your job, your students, or both?

Many instructors will describe teaching as something they are passionate about doing and it stems from a desire to share knowledge and the experience they have acquired, while also helping students develop the necessary academic skill sets, along with improved self-motivation, self-confidence, and overall sense of self-empowerment. Another reason for teaching is a love of learning and this is aligned with the work any educator, which requires ongoing professional self-development and a need to stay current in the field related to the subject that they teach.

Inspired to Share Knowledge

Do you find that you have a desire to share your knowledge and background with adult students? Most college instructors are working in a field related to their classes and they also have advanced education related to the subject matter. This adds depth to the class discussions because they understand the course concepts and can translate theory in a way that allows students to view it within the context of the real world.

The knowledge an educator possesses helps to strengthen all learning activities because it becomes easier to tell if students are on the right track with their comprehension of the course topics. This is demonstrated through student responses during class discussions, along with their written assignments, research, analyses, and other projects. For example, students with limited academic experience often discuss business issues from a "should" or "needs to" perspective, without considering the potential implications or reality of their proposed solutions. Through the use of Socratic questioning and feedback an educator is able to guide students in the right direction and encourage them to explore alternative viewpoints, opinions, and perspectives.

Inspired to Teach Self-Development

As an educator, do you have a desire to help students do something more in class than acquire content-specific knowledge? Do you see students as individuals who have an interest in learning about their personal or professional needs? As any instructor knows, there isn't a set of characteristics or qualities that can be applied to all students because they each possess an individualized approach to learning and they have a variety of skills and abilities. The process of teaching involves being able to quickly assess and interpret where each student is at, from an academic skill set perspective, and knowing how to assist them. This is applicable to any classroom environment, whether in a college or corporate training class.

Working with students requires patience, emotional intelligence, and strong communication skills if you are going to connect with them and develop productive working relationships. Your ability to connect with students is important no matter what the class length may be, whether two hours or ten weeks. Helping students develop skills such as writing and critical thinking can be very rewarding because you watch a shift in their perspective and approach to interacting with their environment, along with the course materials or other information received.

As students discover their capacity to learn they often become more self-confident and over time their self-motivation increases. This is the essence of self-empowerment, when students understand that their work and effort produces a positive result, which includes the accomplishment of their goals. Those goals may be relatively simple, such as successfully completing the class or meeting the learning outcomes, or it can be more complex and involve the acquisition of knowledge or a new skill.

Inspired by Lifelong Learning

Do you have a love of learning? Another reason why someone would choose to work as an educator is a passion for their career field and they enjoy reading current research, topics, and trends related to their chosen field. As an educator it is absolutely essential to stay up-to-date so that your instructional approach relates to current thinking in the field.

Another area of lifelong learning that is necessary for all educators is the continued self-improvement of their instructional strategies. This can be accomplished by reading books, articles, and online resources that are related to adult learning theories and adult education in general. A passion for acquiring and sharing knowledge will help you become a much more effective educator and it can also teach your students how they can become lifelong learners.

Inspired by Your Own Professional Development

As an educator you will find it beneficial for your career and your students to nurture a desire to perform your very best in class, know where you excel in your classroom facilitation strategies, and what areas you need to work on. Take time to look for professional networking opportunities as a means of sharing ideas and resources, and find classes or webinars you can attend to further your continued self-development.

As you review the reasons why you are inspired to teach you are likely to think about the sense of personal and professional fulfillment that results from helping students reach their academic goals. While the work of an educator often requires a substantial investment of time it is part of the process of teaching that you accept as being necessary for the benefit of your students. The opportunity to share your knowledge and experience, while teaching self-development skills, can be transformative for you and your students. When you feel inspired it will bring out the best in your instructional abilities, along with the best performance of your students.

Every Educator Needs a Teaching Philosophy

As an educator, what would you want to say about yourself if you were asked to explain your teaching philosophy? Many online teaching job postings ask candidates to submit a teaching philosophy statement as part of the evaluation process.

You may be surprised, and perhaps you are included in this category, with the number of educators who either do not have a teaching philosophy or cannot articulate clearly and concisely provide (without the use of clichés or generalizations about teaching) any indicator of their own beliefs about learning or teaching.

I have interviewed many faculty for adjunct online teaching positions and most of the candidates I've spoken with have not developed a clearly defined philosophy statement or never thought it was needed. While that does not automatically disqualify them from a teaching position it does not help them provide a true representation of their beliefs about teaching and learning.

Every educator needs a teaching philosophy statement. This is a summary that allows someone else (especially a recruiter or someone in a position to hire new faculty) to develop insight into their teaching and instructional strategies, methods, and practices.

I've seen two different approaches used for those educators who have a well-defined statement; one that is researched-based and one that is very personal and written in the first person. If you are pursuing a new position, my recommendation is that you chose the latter approach and present an overview that represents you as an educator.

What follows is a condensed version of philosophy statement I have used, to help you get started or review what you have already developed.

Conceptualization of Learning

There is a five-part approach that was developed by Nancy Chism, a former Director of Faculty and TA Development at the Ohio State University, which is very helpful for educators. The first part is called Conceptualization of Learning and it is meant for an educator to describe what they believe about learning based upon their knowledge, expertise, education, and experience.

Since my primary work is focused on distance learning, my view of learning is concerned with how students learn in a virtual environment. For online learning, it is my belief that the basic principles of adult education do not change. However, the format of learning has changed and that is the reason why new and updated instructional strategies must be implemented. In a virtual classroom the process of learning involves the acquisition of knowledge and the development of new skills. In order for knowledge to be acquired and retained in long-term memory, students must have an opportunity to apply what they are studying and given a context for learning that is relevant to their lives and/or careers. The same can be stated for the development of new skills; learning occurs when students are given an opportunity to practice what they are being instructed to learn.

In an online classroom, as with any classroom environment, learning is not a one-time event. Learning also does not occur because an online course shell has been created, an instructor has been assigned to teach the course, and students are enrolled in the class. Learning occurs as a result of students receiving and reading materials, processing the information received in a manner that prompts advanced cognitive skills, and then is applied to and connected with existing ideas, knowledge, and real-world scenarios so that it is retained in long-term memory. The learning process does not stop there as that new knowledge must be recalled later if it is to continue to be retained. This means that students will learn only if the subject and course topics are presented in a meaningful manner, one that requires them to do more than memorize concepts.

Conceptualization of Teaching

The next section of a well-defined philosophy statement is a personal narrative about what it means to teach. For me, it is a perspective about learning in a technologically-enabled classroom.

There are phrases used to distinguish traditional classroom teaching from online teaching and includes "sage on the stage" and "guide on the side". I prefer to view online teaching from another perspective. I've read three primary words used to describe the role of the online educator and it includes instructor, facilitator, and teacher. I believe that an online educator must know how to instruct or implement instructional strategies as a function of classroom management.

An online educator must also know how to facilitate a learning process and teach the subject matter through his or her expertise and experience. Within the online classroom an educator must work to see students individually and with unique developmental needs. They must be responsive to their students, available, and easily accessible. They can teach, guide, and mentor students with every interaction, every classroom post, and all of their communication with students.

Goals for Students

The next section that follows needs to be a personal perspective about the goals or expectations that an instructor holds about their students.

For many online schools, the classes have been developed by someone other than the instructor who is assigned to teach the course. That doesn't mean an instructor cannot have their own expectations of students, even if they cannot alter or make additions to the course syllabus. An online educator can state their expectations in classroom announcements and/or through the feedback provided to students.

What I expect students to do, and I support their attempts to do so, is to accomplish more than report what they have read. I want them to work with the course topics, conduct research when needed, investigate subjects that interest them, and when it comes to posting a discussion message or submitting a written assignment, I want them to demonstrate critical thinking.

What this means is that they do more than state a general opinion or belief and instead, they write a well-researched statement or position about the topic. I encourage students to comprehend what they have read, analyze the information, and then apply it in some manner to their personal or professional lives. I show students that I value their ideas, solutions, proposals, and analyses.

Implementation of the Philosophy

This next section provides an overview of how the philosophy is put into practice and it shares insight into an educator's instructional practice.

My philosophy of online teaching has been influenced by my work as an online student and educator, and it continually evolves through my interactions with students and other educators. While I may not be able to be involved in the process of developing every course I'm teaching, I can develop instructional practices that influence how students learn. For example, when I am involved in online discussions I will acknowledge something the student has written, build upon it through my own expertise and experience, and then ask a follow up question that helps to continue to move the conversation forward.

When I provide feedback, I approach that as an opportunity to teach students and I'll use the same approach as my discussion posts and it aligns with Socratic questioning techniques. I want to prompt their intellectual curiosity and encourage them to learn.

With most online classes I have a short period of time to connect with students and my approach is to try to build connections and nurture productive working relationships. I am aware of the tone of my messages, especially since words represent me in an online classroom. I also demonstrate empathy for those students who have low motivation and may be academically under-prepared. When I observe students who are struggling or disengaging from the class, I'll perform outreach attempts to try to help engage them back into the course and address their developmental needs. With every student I acknowledge their efforts and encourage their continued progress, while always being readily available and easily accessible.

Professional Growth Plan

The last component of a well-developed philosophy statement is an overview of how an educator plans to continue their own professional development. Many schools have a professional development requirement and this statement can demonstrate a willingness to continue to learn.

I consider myself to be a lifelong learner and that my learning did not stop once I completed my last formal degree. I continue to learn through my work with online faculty development as the discourse that I have with other faculty allows me to gain new perspectives about learning and teaching. I also continue to research the field that I am actively involved in, which is distance learning, along with other topics of interest that include critical thinking and andragogy.

I am a writer and I have authored numerous articles that are based upon my work and research. My work with instructional design and curriculum development projects has also allowed me to grow professionally as I have expanded my knowledge and skills. I also utilize social media as a means of sharing knowledge, ideas, and resources with a global educator base.

Finally, I work to make scholarly contributions to this field. The two milestones reached to date include publishing a journal article and presenting my research at an international conference for distance learning.

What is Your Philosophy?

Whether or not you have developed a clear position about learning and teaching for your chosen field, now is the time to consider what you believe and the strategies you use - even if you are not seeking another position. Establishing a well-formed statement allows you to reflect upon your current practice and it will help you identify what is working well and areas that you can develop further.

Every educator has a potential to continue to grow and learn, and developing a clear understanding of your beliefs and progress now will allow you to build from your strengths and strengthen your teaching practice. A teaching philosophy is a personal representation of who you are as an educator and something you can use to create developmental plans.

End of Chapter Check-In

What Have You Learned?

What Are Your Strengths?

What Are Your Developmental Areas?

What Will You Apply to Your Teaching Practice?

CHAPTER 10.
EXCELLENCE IN ONLINE TEACHING

How to Develop Excellence in Online Teaching

Instructors who teach online classes know what it is like to work in a virtual environment, along with the challenges that are possible while teaching in this type of classroom. From a lack of interactions that are normally found in a traditional classroom, which connects students to their class and creates a sense of community, to developing relationships with students you cannot see, online teaching requires relational-based instructional strategies, communicating through the use of written rather than spoken words, and an active presence that encourages students to be engaged and highly motivated.

With an online class there will likely be a wide variety of students so it is not possible to always know how to facilitate it in a manner that keeps them fully involved and performing to the very best of their potential.

Being an effective online instructor begins by meeting the required contractual facilitation requirements, while nurturing conditions that address the developmental needs of students and prompt active learning. But meeting the minimum requirements doesn't ensure that a class will function as well as it can as faculty contracts and handbooks are focused on classroom management, along with policies and procedures.

To become an instructor who effectively educates students requires striving for excellence in all aspects of teaching, holding yourself accountable to high standards of expectations, and maintaining excellence even when faced with challenges that are due to class conditions, students, or the demands of balancing numerous responsibilities. Excellence in online teaching is not a permanent state, it is a condition that must be developed, nurtured, and sustained through proactive instructional strategies.

The Importance of Balancing Responsibilities

Teaching effectiveness requires a significant investment of time. There are specific tasks that need to be accomplished each week and to do so a well-balanced schedule is needed. This means that tasks needs to be prioritized so that deadlines are not missed. Some responsibilities require frequent attention, such as maintaining relationships and overseeing class discussions.

Whenever a student issue does arise it can take up planned time and cause some other duties to be pushed back. If classroom management becomes a low priority it can have a negative impact or influence on the performance of your students. What can save time is the development of a proactive plan for completing the required duties and establishing productive work habits.

What Do Students Expect?

Students hold pre-existing expectations about their involvement in the learning process as they begin a class, whether or not those expectations are realistic in nature. They usually expect and/or hope that their new class will be interesting, their instructor will be highly involved and care about their academic progress, and they will be able to complete whatever is required of them. Students usually start from a positive perspective since a new class represents a fresh beginning for them. If this is their first class, it usually represents an important decision that has been made and they will quickly begin to learn the reality of working in an academic environment.

If this is not their first class students may expect to maintain their existing academic progress or if they did not receive an expected outcome from a previous class it still represents hope for change and improvement, either from their own efforts or from an instructor who teaches or grades in a different manner.

As an instructor interacts with their students they may find it challenging to teach in a manner that meets the expectations of every student, especially if they are trying to maintain standards of excellence that students do not understand. While it may not be possible to know what all students expect, an instructor needs to create an engaging environment that is conducive to productive interactions.

Online Teaching Challenges

Online classes are inherently challenging for instructors because they do not begin their classes with a visual and verbal connection. They are challenged to develop and maintain a highly engaged presence through the use of digital communication if they are able to keep the class on track and students moving forward academically. Then there is the challenge of reading a large number of discussion question responses and participation posts, and then developing substantive replies that move the conversations forward.

Feedback is another demanding requirement that is directly tied to students' progress and their developmental needs. Those challenges are the same for every class and over time instructors learn how to address them in an effective manner. However, student issues present a different set of challenges and may become more difficult to address or resolve when students hide behind anonymity and feel free to say whatever they like.

Developing Online Teaching Excellence

The following strategies represent an approach to online teaching that will help you to achieve excellence and become more than an average instructor, which is essential for the development of your work and the performance of your students.

If you embrace a goal to work to excel in how you teach and as you do, your students will benefit from those practices. The approach you develop needs to be a combination of the standards that are put into place by your school and the standards you establish for yourself, while holding yourself accountable to these practices with every class you teach.

#1. Transform Difficult Students

When you have students who are challenging and difficult to work with the best strategy is not to just work with or address them and instead, try to transform them so they become cooperative and highly productive.

As an example, if a student contacts you and doesn't express themselves in the most appropriate manner, use this as a teaching opportunity and then try to get to the heart of the issue. It is possible that they are frustrated, their expectations were not met, they didn't receive the expected outcome, or any other number of possible reasons.

If you can maintain your emotional intelligence throughout your interactions you'll help them become more receptive, which allows you to turn a negative interaction into a potentially productive conversation. You'll also find that a conversation by phone, rather than a series of email exchanges, can also help to build a new relationship.

#2. Get to Know Your Students

It can fairly easy to think of an online class as a collective group rather than as individual students because you do not see them individually in a traditional classroom. But it is possible to get to know your students, from an academic perspective, if you are actively involved in the class and watch their progress. Over time you will know when they are engaged and when it seems that they are beginning to withdraw from the class, and that's when you can take action.

You can begin to learn about your students from the introduction they post if you have that built into your class and it can provide you with insight into their goals and interests. This gives you a sense of what motivates them and if they are facing any existing challenges, whether personally or professionally. Your ability to know your students also helps to inform the feedback you develop and it encourages you to provide customized instruction rather than canned comments.

#3. Develop and Nurture Productive Relationships

Teaching is relational in nature and the development of relationships with students takes time and is often the result of positive interactions. To develop productive relationships, you need to be seen as approachable and willing to provide assistance at all times.

If you make the extra effort with students, they will begin to see you as a real person and that helps them feel comfortable asking you questions. This also builds a sense of acceptance of your instruction, which is especially important when you provide feedback. You can accomplish this through open dialogue and offering multiple forms of contact. It is possible through your efforts to turn virtual connections into a working relationship that helps connect students to their class.

#4. Maintain Professional Communication

Every form of communication that you use with students needs to be thought about from the perspective of its ability to connect with students in a positive manner. Keep in mind the basic process of communication and how the message you send, either directly to a student or as a reply to a message received, will be interpreted once it has been received. What is also subject to interpretation is the tone of the message so the choice of words used matters at all time.

Be certain to manage the mechanics of what you write, which includes being professional, respectful, and willing to help. In other words, offer to assist your students rather than state something such as "see the syllabus" - if you want them to reach out to you again.

Of course that doesn't mean your tone has to be without warmth as the inclusion of welcoming language will help to create a sense of a personality. It is important to maintain this approach even when challenged, and always be willing to follow up with students so there are no unresolved issues.

#5. Establish Your Credibility as an Instructor

This is an aspect of teaching that isn't thought of as a task to be put on a to-do list yet it is a powerful aspect of instruction that determines whether students will trust and respect your position. Credibility cannot be forced and instead it is developed one interaction at a time. Students look to you as the one who is responsible for guiding them and they also expect to be treated fairly.

It is possible to develop a credible reputation by upholding the rules and being fair by listening to your students, understanding their needs, and being flexible whenever possible or warranted. If students believe they have a supportive relationship with you they will be more likely to accept your response to a request, even if it wasn't the outcome expected. It is also important to remember that one negative interaction can interrupt the progress you've made with your students and that is why all interactions you have matter for your teaching presence.

#6. Establish High Expectations

One method of creating standards of excellence is to establish high expectations for your students and yourself. This involves holding yourself accountable for the quality of all aspects of the work you do and establishing yourself as a role model and example for students to follow. As an instructor you can hold an expectation that students will provide substantive work, be willing to learn, maintain academic standards of excellence, and also meet the standards established by the school. To accomplish this goal, you must do more than facilitate a class and check off each requirement, you must also be open to following those same guidelines.

#7. Maintain a Proactive Approach

If you are paying attention to your class and monitoring students' progress, you know when to intervene whenever you observe a student who is off track. This is a student who is falling off the radar, who is not participating in discussions, and/or may not be completing their assignments. The best approach for this type of student is to maintain outreach contact attempts until they respond in some manner.

The purpose of these outreach attempts is to show them that they are valued and you want to assist them. The hope is that with supportive outreach attempts you can get them back on the right course. But if they don't respond, what do you do? The answer is to not give up and encourage them to contact to you through every option that you have established, including a phone call. You should also explore other options made available by your school, which could include notifying the student's academic advisor.

#8. Develop a Supportive Mindset

Your support is needed to nurture a growth mindset within your students. This helps to determine if they will persist and continue when faced with challenges or quit and give up. There are going to be many instances when students will challenge this mindset. For example, if you have a student who does not see the need to change and will not read or utilize the feedback provided.

One approach that you can take is to be very specific in the feedback provided and never change your willingness to be concerned with their academic needs and ability to learn. Within that feedback you can ask questions and encourage a dialogue with them, while using positive encouragement as a motivational tool. If you can be supportive you will establish a connection so that they eventually come to realize that the feedback provided is personalized and meant to help them.

Remember Why You Teach

From my perspective as an educator, I want to inspire students to discover their capabilities, their ability to learn and grow, and connect with the subject matter in a meaningful way. Many online educators have also expressed a desire to make a difference in the lives of their students, cultivate classroom conditions that prompt learning, grow professionally, and share their knowledge and expertise with students.

As you review the reasons why you are inspired to teach you are likely to think about the sense of personal and professional fulfillment that results from helping students reach their academic goals. While the work of an educator often requires a substantial investment of time it is part of the process of teaching that you accept as being necessary for the benefit of your students.

When you feel inspired it will bring out the best in your instructional abilities, along with the best performance of your students. The ongoing practice of striving for excellence in your work as an online instructor, or becoming more than average, will ultimately be transformative for you and your students.

Maintaining Excellence When Challenged

Online classes can be rewarding if students are highly engaged, self-motivated, and performing to the best of their capabilities. What makes online teaching challenging is the lack of visual cues, which means an instructor does not have the benefit of visually assessing students as they attempt to complete the learning activities and other course requirements.

That's not the only challenge an online instructor may face. There may be technological issues with the online classroom platform or challenges related to managing a class while meeting the facilitation requirements. What makes online teaching even more challenging are difficult students, which includes students who don't seem to review their feedback and are unreceptive to constructive criticism, along with students who fail to communicate in a respectful tone. Working with difficult students usually requires spending additional time and may create feelings of frustration for the instructor, especially if the students are not responsive.

Even if an instructor is highly visible and engaged in their online class, and offers multiple methods of contact for students, it still may be difficult to pinpoint the underlying causes of student issues. Inappropriate communication must be addressed right away through corrective methods; however, knowing something about the student and the reason for their frustrations can have a positive impact on the situation.

Unfortunately, some students rely upon anonymity and do not respond to outreach attempts. Online students are known primarily through their classroom posts, papers, and messages, which means an instructor may not learn much about them if they are not actively involved in the class - and that makes understanding their developmental needs much more challenging. There are methods an instructor can use as part of their instructional practice to work with difficult students, which means that excellence in online teaching can be maintained during the best and worst of classroom circum-stances.

Don't Let Time Be an Issue

A majority of online classes are taught by adjunct instructors. This means that those instructors who are teaching these classes are likely maintaining other responsibilities, similar to their students. Also like their students they may have a specific amount of time devoted for involvement in their classes and when they are online and working there are specific tasks that must be accomplished.

Every instructor hopes that students will be highly motivated, fully present when they are in class, and have a mindset that is receptive towards learning. The reality is that students aren't always performing in that manner or have a positive disposition. Whenever a student issue does arise it can cause some facilitation duties to be pushed back. While it is not possible to predict when student issues will occur, an instructor can develop a time management plan for completing the required duties, and have additional time built in to address developmental needs and challenges.

Consider the Perspective of Your Students

Students usually begin their classes from a positive perspective because it represents a fresh start. They hope that their new class will be interesting and their instructor is either the same as the last class, or different if the outcome was not what they had expected. This underscores the reason why challenges sometimes arise as students have an expectation about their involvement in the learning process and a perception about how their instructors should also be involved in the class. As students work on the required tasks or learning activities they will utilize the same work habits from the last class and continue to perform in their most current pattern of productivity.

If students are open to feedback and constructive criticism, their work method and approach to formulating their posts and papers will become adaptable when needed as a means of self-improvement. However, for those students who hold a belief that they know best how to perform or believe they are performing their best and that is adequate now, they are likely to feel challenged by anything their instructors have to say as they provide feedback. How those students respond determines their involvement in class as it progresses, and they always have a choice - they can maintain appropriate control of their classroom behavior or become uncooperative.

Online Teaching Challenges

Online classes are inherently challenging for instructors because there is no visual and verbal connection. They must maintain a highly engaged presence if they are able to keep the class on track. There is also a challenge of reading students' discussion question posts and developing substantive replies.

Feedback is another demanding requirement that is directly tied to students' progress and developmental needs. Those challenges are the same for every class and over time instructors learn how to address them in an effective manner. But student issues are the challenges that may be more difficult to address and resolve. It is very easy for a student to hide behind anonymity and believe they are free to say whatever they like.

It seems there is a growing trend among students, those who do not communicate in an appropriate manner and become aggressive, hostile, uncooperative, or defensive. There was a time when a non-responsive student was my biggest challenge as an online educator. Now I find there are students who express their feelings in an unprofessional manner. I'm still surprised when that happens as I reflect upon the time when I was an online student and during that time I would not communicate with an instructor in an unprofessional manner. But it seems that some students will establish their beliefs and expectations about learning and refuse to change. It is situations like this that requires proactive instructional strategies.

Methods to Address Students

Every educator needs a set of strategies that have been thought out in advance, as a means of addressing students who need additional assistance or present challenges. Often you may not know what the best solution is until you have addressed a unique challenge or situation for the very first time.

Students Who Don't Respond:

If you are actively involved in your class and monitoring students' progress, you know when to intervene should you observe a student who is off track or not making progress. You hope that with supportive outreach attempts you can help get them back on the right course. But if they don't respond, what do you do? The answer is to not give up and encourage them to contact to you through every option that you will allow or have established, including a phone call.

Uncooperative Students:

This is a student who will not respond to any request that you have made. It doesn't matter how small or significant the request was, you had a reason for making it. If the student is uncooperative the best approach is to send a message to them and ask for a reply. In addition, ask for a contact appointment and express your interest in their development and progress in class. The purpose is to neutralize any negative emotions that may arise within you or your students.

Students Who Are Disengaging:

This is the student who is falling off the radar or slowing withdrawing from the class, who is not actively involved in class discussions, and/or may not be completing their assignments. The best approach for this type of student is to maintain outreach contact attempts until they respond in some manner.

The purpose of these outreach attempts is to show them that they are valued and you want to assist them.

Students Who Are Not Receptive:

This is the student who does not see the need to change and does not seem to read or utilize the feedback provided in any form. One strategy you can implement is to be very specific in the feedback provided and maintain this supportive approach. Within that feedback you can ask questions and encourage a dialogue with them, which demonstrates to students you are reading their work and offering more than canned responses. Try to establish a connection so that they will eventually realize that the personalized feedback provided is meant to help them.

Unprofessional Communication:

This is the student who cannot interact with you without utilizing communication that is unprofessional or unproductive. It may also involve a long series of back-and-forth emails as the student tries to justify their point of view. What you can do in this situation begins by sending a response that demonstrates a caring attitude and willingness to assist them. Offer a phone conversation so that a connection can be made without the use of email. If they decline and continue with their inappropriate communication, remind them of the student code of conduct. You should also follow any established school procedure for contacting other individuals as needed.

Online Teaching Excellence

This is the most important aspect of online teaching - instructors who maintain excellence in their style of facilitation, their interactions with students, and their expectations of students. As an instructor you can hold an expectation that students will provide substantive work, be willing to learn, and also meet the standards that have been established by the school.

To accomplish this goal, you must do more than facilitate a class and check off each requirement, you must also be open to creating conditions that are conducive to learning. And just as you expect of your students, you must be willing to receive constructive feedback and adapt your instructional methods as needed. When you have challenging students, even when you have done your best to create optimal class conditions, you must be prepared to address it quickly and in a receptive manner.

A challenging student is often an indicator of a connection that was never fully established or has now been disrupted. Even if you have already done your best to be supportive, you must do so now even more than ever. Every action you take must be done with the intent of establishing a new or renewed connection. This is not about what students will state on their end-of-course evaluations, it is about reaching out and getting through to a student who is stuck, withdrawn, or unable to be involved in the learning process with an open mind.

It is up to you to demonstrate your willingness to support their progress. Will it always work? Probably not; however, if you have done your part and offered to assist them you will either see a gradual change or they will continue to struggle. No matter what, never give up your coaching attempts and determination to achieve excellence in online teaching - even with the most challenging students or circumstances.

Rewards of Online Teaching

As an online instructor, what would you list if you were asked to consider the benefits of being responsible for teaching a class?

When you are facilitating an online class it may be easy to first recognize the challenges that are possible, which may include the time commitment required to manage the class and meet your required facilitation duties.

Online teaching can also be very rewarding when you consider the transformative nature of classroom facilitation, your ability to influence the process of learning, and the opportunities for professional growth that it provides.

The Transformative Power of Teaching

You hold an ability to transform your students through a responsive approach to classroom facilitation, one that encourages and inspires students to reach for their full potential, especially when you can see students for who they can become, instead of reinforcing who they are now. Through your interactions with students you can instill confidence, teach discipline with a structured classroom, lead through your example, and develop working relationships as a teacher and a mentor.

Students know that they will receive some form of feedback for their work and they look for your response and direction. You can create a supportive environment, one that helps students with their developmental needs, by providing them with specific resources. Students also have professional needs and through their participation in the class, along with your guidance, they can develop skill sets that will help prepare them for a career or career advancement. Watching students make progress throughout the class can be very rewarding as it is often a reflection of their response to your facilitation techniques.

You Can Influence Learning

You can establish conditions in the classroom that create a learning environment. Through your classroom participation you can help bring the course materials to life, add your expertise to the discussions, and guide students through focused learning where they are developing critical thinking skills and creating new knowledge. What can make this process of learning rewarding is that you have an ability to acknowledge your students' contributions, help them apply knowledge to the real world, and assist them as they work through ideas and interact with information provided throughout the course.

Opportunities for Professional Growth

As you facilitate online classes over time you begin to learn teaching methods that are effective and methods of building rapport with your students. The online classroom requires you to utilize words in a way that establishes a connection and a meaningful classroom presence.

This can be rewarding when you reflect upon previous classes and what has worked well, realizing that it is possible to create conditions that result in effective interactions, along with professional development of your students and your own facilitation practice. Professional growth may also result from learning through the experiences of your students and discovering ways of meeting their needs. Many schools also require instructors to seek out professional developmental opportunities such as continuing education courses and workshops.

Facilitating an online class can be challenging; however, you can choose to focus on the demands of your time in the process of being an effective instructor or you can remember the potential rewards and use that as a source of motivation to create and sustain a transformative learning environment. Every class you facilitate provides a new opportunity to connect with students, experience professional growth, and have a direct impact on their academic journey.

End of Chapter Check-In

What Have You Learned?

What Are Your Strengths?

What Are Your Developmental Areas?

What Will You Apply to Your Teaching Practice?

CHAPTER 11.
WORKING AS AN ONLINE INSTRUCTOR

The Work of an Online Instructor

When I began my career in the field of distance learning in 2005, there were significantly more jobs than qualified instructors. Then there was a gradual shift because of the growing number of people who either completed advanced education or believed they are well-suited for working in this environment. The idea of working from home, rather than teach in a traditional college classroom, became quite appealing. While the number of schools offering online courses and degree programs increased, that did not always mean the number of instructors needed also increased. There were more schools competing for the potential base of students and that caused enrollment to level out across the industry.

Now there is another shift occurring in the field of distance learning. There have been changes with regards to regulating the for-profit industry and as a result some schools have seen enrollment numbers drop and others have closed. This has reduced the number of online teaching opportunities, making this type of work highly competitive.

There are other considerations for those who want to teach online. First, most online teaching positions are filled through the use of adjuncts. There are very few full time positions and most adjuncts are generally placed in a pool without a guarantee of receiving a class at any time. Adjuncts are assigned classes according to the number of students enrolled and when enrollment is down, instructors are no longer needed.

Another important factor for obtaining work as an online instructor is the education requirement stated in many of the job ads. While many of the online teaching positions used to accept a master's degree as the minimum qualification, there is a growing number of schools that now require a doctorate degree for teaching both undergraduate and graduate courses. With a smaller number of available positions, and a shift in the minimum educational qualification, it has become difficult for many instructors to find work - especially those who have a master's degree as their highest level of education.

For anyone who wants to be in this role and develop a long term career, there needs to be a focus on the responsibilities of this position and how to best be prepared.

Common Frustrations and Challenges

As an online educator and faculty development specialist it is fairly easy for me to put together a list of frustrations and challenges. An adjunct generally will not be provided with any benefits and that includes vacation time. Many adjuncts will take their work with them if they are on vacation, or schedule a break between classes. But there are more significant issues. Something that is becoming more common has to do with experienced adjuncts being passed over for full-time positions, leaving those instructors with the sense that they are not valued. From an economic standpoint it seems that the rationale by for-profit schools is that it is less expensive to hire inexperienced educators.

In addition, many adjuncts who find jobs listed also experience frustration when they try to apply for those limited positions. There's nothing worse than getting the dreaded email from human resources that praises the applicant for their extensive experience but they have not been considered for the position, often without a phone call to discuss their background or qualifications. What is unfortunate about both of these issues is that experienced online educators can start an online class and be able to hit the ground running or quickly facilitate the class without significant advanced training.

For many adjuncts they quickly realize that they are considered to be an instructor of last resort, which means they are not offered courses until the full-time faculty have met their requirements, or enrollment spikes create additional opportunities. It is becoming increasingly difficult for adjuncts to plan a work schedule more than a couple of weeks in advance because they can sit on the sidelines and not be offered a course until the very last moment.

In addition, the industry standard for adjuncts has changed as well. Most schools paid adjuncts on a per class basis but now some online schools are determining payment on a per student basis, and without compensation for the prep time required. If an adjunct is assigned a class with just a handful of students, and they are paid on a per student basis, they could realistically make less than minimum wage over the duration of the course.

Typical Working Conditions

Most adjuncts are given a list of required duties and expectations regarding their performance in the class, which is fairly standard among online universities. Flexibility is one of the key advantages provided and that allows an adjunct to work around a full-time job or other responsibilities. Many adjuncts will continue to accept classes believing that they need to retain an active status, which means they may accept classes with low enrollment and potentially low pay.

Most universities also have required training, usually during the initial recruitment stage and as part of ongoing professional development. That training is usually unpaid, even if the initial training session lasts up to four weeks. What most adjuncts will state when asked about working conditions is that it is unpredictable, they have no control over course offerings, there are long work hours expected, there are significant demands, and high expectations for performance.

Another aspect of online teaching that some view as a benefit and others a disadvantage is that classes for most online schools are pre-built, which means the materials and learning activities have already been developed and that minimizes the need to invest in additional prep time.

Expert Advice for Online Instructors

Whether you are a new or experienced online instructor, there are some basics that can prepare as you develop your instructional practice. I recommend that you review your instructional approach at the end of each class to determine if it is still highly effective.

#1. Establish a Productive Work Habit

One of the most important strategies necessary for any online adjunct involves time management. Most adjuncts work from home and either wait until the end of the week to complete their facilitation duties or they have an always-on syndrome, believing they must be present in the class at all times. It is therefore necessary to establish a set routine and allocate time specifically for facilitation duties throughout the week, which will help you to develop productive work habits. To maximize your time, and meet all of the required facilitation duties, take each duty and allocate time for it throughout the week.

#2. Establish a Virtual Presence

An instructional presence is another vital component of online teaching. This involves being available to answer questions and address concerns, maintaining a disposition of responsiveness to students, and posting messages frequently in class discussions. A virtual classroom presence means you are actively and interactively involved in the class and with your students.

A virtual presence is established as a well-planned and developed instructional strategy. All communication and posts need to be well thought out, planned for in advance, carefully constructed, and meaningful for the learning process. When feedback is provided it should be focused on the mechanics and content of what was written, along with the student's overall developmental progress. Participation in class discussions needs to involve more than reactive responses and includes the use of credible, relevant, and timely, academic sources. Many instructors also find it helpful to create their own resources, especially introductory videos and presentations that enhance student learning.

#3. Engage in Professional Development

Ongoing professional development is another strategy that online instructors need to proactively manage and plan for ahead of time. Since most online schools have an annual requirement they may offer workshops and seminars that can be of benefit, or at least meet the minimum requirement.

What I have discovered as a faculty class reviewer is that having subject matter expertise or work experience in particular field does not mean that an instructor is fully capable of facilitating a learning process. This is where learning about adult education theories and sound instructional strategies can be beneficial for career development. As an instructor takes webinars, work-shops, or online classes they should remember to add this continuing education to their resume, along with links to professional social media accounts to demonstrate an ongoing commitment to lifelong learning.

Online Teaching Can Be Rewarding

As an online educator I find it very rewarding when I can observe that learning has occurred, which means there were students that were receptive to the learning process, they wrote well, and they were highly engaged and motivated.

I've also found that the inherent challenges for work as an adjunct can be overcome through dedication to this position and the development of your teaching methods. Those instructors who are highly engaged and effective do this type of work because they want to be involved in the process of transformational learning and they enjoy the facilitation requirements, even when there is a significant time requirements involved.

While it may seem that there are limited opportunities for adjuncts, there will be positions available for those who have transformed from instructors to distinguished educators and scholar practitioners, which means they are highly trained, educated, and motivated. Adjuncts are valuable commodities for the field of distance learning, especially those who care about their work and their performance in the online classroom.

Creating a Work Life Balance

A majority of online instructors work as adjuncts and that means they may also be balancing other responsibilities. They know that managing their time is extremely important and that their weekdays may be spent just managing the basics. There are other priorities that include involvement in weekly discussions, answering questions, and completing required feedback. While instructors are required to post their participation messages on a fixed number of days, the level of students' engagement in those discussion depends upon their active involvement. That may mean that the task of reviewing papers may have to wait until the weekend.

The demand of maintaining this pace for the facilitation of a class is rigorous and often leaves little time or flexibility to slow down. Of course one solution is to not accept new course offerings but there is always an underlying concern that the number of classes offered may decline. The potential problem for this type of work cycle is that eventually something will have to give. An instructor may reach a point of being burned out and/or their work performance may begin to suffer. What every online instructor needs to do is to create a balance between their work schedule and their personal life.

Demands of Online Teaching

While the scenario presented may not sound very enticing to someone who anticipates working in this field, it is a reality based upon the nature of an online class. This is relevant for someone who works full time and then teaches part-time as an adjunct. You can leave your class unattended for a day or two, depending upon the contractual requirements; however, you then need to consider if checking in is worth the time so the class is well-managed. You also need to decide if you are content with minimal involvement in the class or if you would like to provide the best possible classroom learning experience.

As an example, you may be required to only post 10 participation messages and you have a class with 20 students. Will you decide to post 10 messages or will you respond to every student at least once to engage and guide them? In addition, do you want to provide minimally adequate feedback or do you want to devote the time necessary to provide substantive and meaningful feedback? All of these choices will have a direct impact on the amount of time you will decide to devote to your class. These are factors that should be considered before you accept a new class offering.

What is a Work Life Balance?

The answer to this question may seem obvious - allow time for both as they are equally important. This is true to a certain extent for most people; however, there are varying degrees of importance and that is what you need to sort out as you establish a working philosophy. I am certain everyone would agree that no one can work long hours and remain highly productive. This means you will need to factor in some down time every week, which may include time to exercise, go for walk, unplug from technology, or spend time with family and friends.

I've observed a common problem among online instructors and that is being tethered to technology, more specifically email and

Internet sources. Some people cannot disengage until they go to sleep at night and this is typical for those who have a very demanding work schedule. If this is you, it may be necessary to decline a course offering if you are feeling overworked or overwhelmed. In other words, you need to establish some type of balance as you consider the frequency of when you will be available to teach.

Warning Signs of Overload

One of the very first indicators that you are becoming overloaded is how you feel. If you have too much to do and you are tired, or you do not have the time to do the things that you want to do, you may likely experience feelings of frustration or anxiety. If those feelings are left unchecked or not well-managed it may manifest as a negative attitude, tone, or disposition towards your work.

Besides your feelings, which are always in important indicator, there are other warning signs that can show up. For example, there may be missed requirements such as returning feedback to students after it was due, or any deviation from your normal teaching style or philosophy regarding how you want to teach. It may begin with a missed duty and progress into negative emotions and feeling unappreciated, underpaid, and the list continues. Any time there is an indicator like this it means you need to review the work life balance you have established and make adjustments.

Strategies for a Work Life Balance

Establishing a balance requires careful planning and continual monitoring. Below are some strategies that you can utilize to adjust your balance, which are strategies I have used as part of my online teaching practice.

#1. Develop a Working Philosophy

Determine how much time you're willing to devote to your career, both daily and weekly. Also make a determination of how much personal time you would like to have each day and throughout the week.

#2. Establish a Weekly Schedule

Every day make an attempt to allocate time based upon your personal philosophy. This will encourage you to maximize your time and show yourself (and others) that you (and they) are also important in your life. This is a matter of establishing priorities based upon what is important to you.

#3. Don't Make Excuses

Once you determine what is important in your life, instead of what others expect of you, then make a plan and follow through with it. You'll find that trying to please others is not productive but taking care of your needs is. For example, some people are career driven and only need an occasional break to feel well-attuned to an inner sense of well-being and fulfillment. Everyone is different and if you stick with your decision you will find that others around you become supportive because you have established a plan that includes them.

#4. Determine the Value of Your Time

If being an adjunct ensures you have needed income, consider the impact of working all of the time. If you need a break, make that decision and then start cutting corners where you can. In other words, earning money may not be as valuable as maintaining your sense of well-being. In addition, it is very likely that if you are performing well you will continue to receive course offerings.

Maintaining Your Balance

Finding the right work life balance for you is not an exact science, rather it is something you will need to establish and then monitor because there are many variables involved. For example, you may decide to teach another class instead of taking a break due to financial obligations. However, you can establish an agreement with yourself that you will take a break afterwards. Making these types of trade-offs is a form of creating balance - provided that you stick with it. If warning signs are popping up and you ignore them, the consequences could be a poorly managed class or worse - you could develop an adverse reaction to stress.

If you decide to take a break from teaching a class because you haven't had a break in some time, learn to develop the confidence to believe in yourself as an educator. Those online instructors who perform well are the ones who are most likely to receive continued course offerings. If you don't take a needed break it could end up resulting in a negative class outcome.

The point is to understand how important your career and your personal life are to you. There are no right or wrong answers but there is a best plan of action for you based upon how much time you want to devote to each priority. Some people need the income, some teach for fun, some enjoy a busy career, and others value more time with their family. If you have established a philosophy and a proactive plan, you will then be able to focus on all priorities and pay attention to how well you manage each one.

Time Management Strategies

Online instructors understand the need to manage their time effectively. There is much more involved than reviewing papers and participating in class discussions. Managing the demands of a busy class requires an investment of time, energy, and effort for every instructor. Instructors are managing classroom operations, engaging students through discussions, maintaining a supportive learning environment, and completing specific facilitation requirements.

At times it is possible to feel prepared and ready to meet the demands of a busy class, while at other times it may feel as if there is not enough time.

Development of an effective time management plan involves selecting tools and techniques that create an effective approach to completing all required facilitation tasks in a timely and productive manner.

Examine Your Current Schedule

A useful starting point for the development of a time management plan involves conducting a review of the weekly requirements and how those obligations are being met. This is a helpful approach for instructors who already have an effective time management strategy as they can better understand what is working well and maintain that progress.

If this is you, an effective starting point is to keep a record of your time, duties, and classroom activities for at least a week. You can create a log or develop some form of note-taking as you track each day of the week or weeks, depending upon how long you are going to monitor your work.

After the designated time period for monitoring your time has concluded, you can complete your analysis by asking the following questions.

- What requirements were met ahead of schedule, completed by the required due date, or were late?

- How did you feel during the class week and then at the end of the week?

- Were there any periods of stress encountered while meeting these requirements?

- Were there any optional facilitation duties, instructional best practices, or other pending projects that were not completed?

- Is the goal each week to complete the minimal facilitation requirements or should there be more time allotted to exceed the facilitation expectations?

- What were your strengths and areas of development?

Summarize your week by carefully examining what worked well and what did not. This is the most productive method of developing a revised time management plan.

Time Management Strategies

Based upon what you have learned after tracking your time and analyzing the outcomes, you can then decide what strategies would be helpful to better improve the use of your time. You may need to simply fine tune your approach to time management or completely overhaul it.

Possible time management strategies include the following:

Focus on Teaching Goals:

To determine your teaching goals, answer these questions: Is class facilitation an obligation to fulfill each week or is the purpose of facilitation to exceed the required duties and spend additional time developing a more effective learning environment?

Avoid Time Wasters:

Are there any facilitation aspects that would be considered unnecessary busy work? While it seems unlikely that you would engage in any work that takes up more of your time, it is possible you don't recognize time wasters until you've tracked your time for a week or two.

Establish Priorities:

What are the most important tasks each week? Schedule a specific time for working on the facilitation requirements, breaking down large projects into smaller ones that can be easily managed, and schedule the top priorities first.

Work Ahead:

I begin my facilitation duties early in the week to avoid missing deadlines and developing stress. It is a proactive strategy that you may find helpful as well. The primary disadvantage for this approach is that it may feel as if you are spending a lot of time working on your facilitation duties all week long; however, this is offset by feeling in control of your time and not rushed if the unexpected occurs.

Look for Pockets of Time:

A pocket of time occurs any time during the week when you find you have a few minutes or hours that you had nothing planned for or something scheduled was either cancelled or no longer a priority. If you have time like this, you can either use it as downtime or work ahead on another project.

Analyze Use of Time and Energy Levels:

As you are working on your schedule for the week, try to determine the time of day when you are the most productive. For some people it is early in the morning and for others it occurs late at night. If you leverage your peak energy for work on your tasks you will likely increase your productivity.

Be Alert for Procrastination:

This can happen to anyone; setting aside duties that are complex or seem overwhelming - until the very last minute. Organization is the best strategy for avoiding procrastination. If you aren't organized you could easily forget some important duties or tasks, or possibly miss deadlines.

Time Management Tools

Time management tools that can help you organize your week include a calendar, to-do list, or schedule. Some instructors prefer to use a traditional paper planner and others utilize technological tools to stay organized. Whatever your preference may be, find something that will help you be mindful of the tasks that need to be completed so you can stay focused and meet all required deadlines. And if you discover any pockets of unexpected time, use it to review your schedule and work ahead.

Be in Control of Your Time

There are many expectations and requirements in place for your work as an online instructor. Meeting the facilitation duties and deadlines each week can be challenging at times, especially if you are an adjunct instructor. Develop a list that includes everything needed to be completed each week, including any additional projects or time you want to devote to creating a meaningful learning environment. Create a plan that schedules or allocates a specific amount of time for your duties and stay focused on your teaching goals. You will likely feel better prepared and in control of your week so that teaching is enjoyable and you find you are working in a highly productive manner.

Stress Management Strategies

Facilitating a class can be a very demanding process when there are numerous instructional requirements, policies and procedures that must be upheld, and a need to create an environment that is conducive to learning. In addition, adult students have developmental needs and an expectation that their instructor will be present, active, responsive, and engaged in the class.

It can be easy to feel pressure from these many duties and obligations, which in turn may produce stress. Development of a proactive plan to manage the potential for stress is essential for any instructor. There are several techniques provided that may help you to reduce the potential for stress.

Develop a Schedule

Having a regular schedule is an important part of managing stress and many instructors have a schedule that is set by their responsibilities. Facilitation duties can be divided up and scheduled according to personal due dates, along with contractual due dates. It is a good idea to review that schedule on occasion to make sure it is still effective and all facilitation requirements are being addressed.

Time Management & Stress Management

Effective time management is directly related to stress management. If there has been enough time allocated to complete the necessary facilitation duties, you may feel in control of your time and less likely to experience anxiety or stress.

Consider these questions as you review your time management plan:

Do you have any potential time traps that could cause stress? Should you consider or weigh the importance of obligations and activities? How can you plan and prioritize your weekly responsibilities?

Downtime for Renewal

Consider these questions:

Do you believe that downtime should be included in your weekly time management plan? Does downtime help you feel refreshed? How do you remind yourself that you need time to rejuvenate yourself so that you can manage stress?

As you develop and manage your schedule you will likely feel better prepared to meet the required facilitation duties and this in turn will reduce the potential for anxiety and stress. The purpose of downtime is to shift your attention away from the intensity of your schedule long enough to allow you to catch your breath and feel relaxed. That can be a matter of a few minutes or several hours, depending upon what has been allocated in your time management plan.

One method of proactively addressing stress is to consider your overall well-being, which includes your attitude, the way you eat, the method you use to manage your time, and the amount of sleep you get. The better you feel, the more likely you can cope effectively with stressful conditions.

Another method of addressing and eliminating stress is to analyze your energy level throughout the day and consider when you are the most productive. If possible, match the time of day that you have the most energy to the most difficult tasks because they will require the most concentration and focus.

It is unlikely that you can completely eliminate stress. There are going to be times as an instructor when classroom management, deadlines, and student interactions feel manageable and other times when all of these demands become too much. But you don't need to let it get the best of you. Learn to become proactive by recognizing signs and symptoms. Schedule downtime to allow yourself a chance to feel renewed and increase your productivity.

How Stress in Perceived

There is a difference between productive stress and negative stress. A busy schedule with many responsibilities can produce good stress when an effective time management plan is in place, which can help you stay motivated. Negative stress is often a result of feeling there isn't enough time. A key factor is perception.

Everyone has the potential to experience stress in their jobs and their personal lives. The way that this stress is perceived often determines how it is addressed and handled. If you perceive stress as something you can manage and control, you will be able to address it and work with it.

What Triggers Stress

Managing stress effectively is necessary so that you can maximize your effectiveness as an instructor. It is helpful to recognize what triggers the potential for stress. As an example, your physical health and well-being may trigger stress if you are not getting enough rest. One method of identifying potential stress triggers is to keep a journal and monitor the outcome of your facilitation duties and how you felt throughout the week.

Establish Proactive Control

Developing a proactive stress management plan allows you to maintain control of your facilitation duties without feeling overwhelmed. If you control your time and how you feel about the use of your time you are likely to complete your required instructional duties and manage your class effectively.

If you don't control how you spend your time and allow yourself to experience stress, it can have many negative consequences that extend beyond missed deadlines and includes a negative tone in the communication you have with your students. When you move beyond feeling in control and actually taking control of your schedule, you will minimize the potential for stress and negative feelings. This will allow you to better enjoy your teaching and class facilitation duties.

What it Means to Be a Modern Educator

Traditional college instruction is part of a well-established tradition that has remained fairly unchanged over time. Becoming an instructor in this environment has meant conformity to teaching standards that have also remained mostly unchanged.

A college professor is associated with someone who is a subject matter expert, likely to achieve a position with tenure, and have dual roles as an instructor and researcher. It is expected that they will be a published author of scholarly journal articles that have been peer-reviewed and contributed knowledge to their field.

While this form of education and instructor still exists, there is another academic institution that has also been established and it is an online college and university. For this modern form of higher education, you will not likely find any positions that are labeled professor. Most online schools hire adjuncts and many refer to their instructors as facilitators. Some of these schools expect instructors to complete annual professional development requirements but rarely does that include publishing journal articles.

In addition to online schools, many traditional colleges and universities offer online courses and degrees, typically hiring adjuncts to fill those roles. What is needed now is a new category of educator, one that meets the needs of students who participate in this modern form of education. I have referred to this new form of instructor as a Modern Educator.

From Traditional to Online Teaching

The traditional format for educating students is a lecture-driven class. An instructor delivers information to students and they must demonstrate what was learned through assessments that include quizzes and exams. They know that their instructor or professor is an expert in the particular subject area for their class.

This method of instruction is the same style that is used in primary education and it is teacher-centered. As technology brought new possibilities for the field of education a new format developed - online courses and online degrees. At first traditional educators taught these courses but over time that approach has changed, especially as adjuncts filled a majority of the instructional roles. Now that online schools having been fully established in the education field, a new type of educator has also emerged.

Evolution to Modern Teaching

With the growth of online learning came the need for hiring a large volume of instructors. Some online universities offer classes that begin weekly and others have monthly start dates. Hiring adjuncts was the answer and the majority of jobs teaching undergraduate students have been filled by instructors holding a master's degree in the subject field they were teaching. Over time the number of instructors qualified to teach online grew substantially and now many adjunct positions require a doctorate degree.

What contributed to the increased pool of available online instructors is the fluctuation in enrollment numbers, the limited number of full-time online instructor positions, and the increase in degree specializations - especially those related to teaching with technology. It is estimated that there are nearly two million adjunct instructors teaching online courses.

Modern educators are also different from a college professor through the manner in which they are allowed to present themselves in the classroom. An online instructor is often called a facilitator and rarely is this position referred to as a professor - although some instructors will refer to themselves as a professor to establish a position of authority in the learning process. Many online schools tell their instructors to use their first name as a means of creating a casual and approachable image, even if the instructor has earned a doctorate degree.

An Example of a Modern Educator

Within the field of online education there is a significant difference among educator types. There are those with a master's degree who can teach undergraduate courses and those with doctorate degrees who can teach both undergraduate and graduate students.

My work as an educator has evolved from traditional college teaching to that of online teaching and now I have become a Modern Educator. Instead of spending months (or possibly longer) trying to become published in a scholarly journal, I publish online articles. This doesn't mean that I do not value publishing in traditional formats as I have a published journal article and a traditional print book. I have also made a presentation at a professional conference.

However, instead of my work being available only to those who have access to and read scholarly journals, I now have an opportunity to reach a broader audience. My work is available as soon as I write and publish it, and more importantly I understand how to use social media. I am connected to an international basis of educators, universities, and students through the use of social media and professional networking websites. Through social media it is possible to share ideas and resources, along with online articles, blog posts, and other intellectual contributions.

This also applies to transformation of the publishing process. Instead of waiting to find a publisher and follow the traditional publishing route, I have self-published some of my books. This has allowed me to become highly engaged in the field of higher education and it has redefined what it means to be a college instructor.

Steps to Becoming a Modern Educator

Whether you have a master's degree or doctorate degree, if you teach online courses you need professional development. But this should be more than taking a workshop; it needs to involve making an intellectual contribution. In addition, the work of a Modern Educator should involve some form of social or professional networking.

Here are some strategies you can use to become a Modern Educator.

#1. Establish a Blog

A blog can provide a platform to share your expertise, share ideas and resources, and summarize your knowledge. As you continue to conduct research for your areas of professional interest you can include what you have learned within your blog posts. There are numerous blog platforms that will allow you to create and share your blog posts at little or no cost.

#2. Write Online Articles

Instead of taking the time required to write and submit articles to scholarly journals, which can always be an option for you, find a resource that allows you to publish online articles. The articles you write, which are based upon your knowledge and experience, will allow you to reach a broader audience, refine your writing skills, and establish yourself as a subject matter expert. I first began by utilizing Ezine Articles, which is an article marketing database. This helped me begin to find an audience. Now I am posting articles on LinkedIn to reach a much broader audience.

#3. Utilize Social Networking

Every online educator needs to learn how to establish their presence through the use of technology. It only makes sense that if you work in a technology-enabled environment you should also know how to be engaged in online communities. LinkedIn provides a means of professional networking, finding groups that match your interest, and even finding online jobs. Twitter can connect you to a global base of educators, students, and similar resources.

#4. Develop a Website

If you find that you are highly ambitious and want to develop more than a blog you could also build your own website. This would be a place for you to house resources that you have created, which could be shared with educators and students. There are free webhosting services available and others that charge a small fee.

#5. Write E-Books

The field of publishing has changed and now authors are taking back control by making their books available in an e-book format. Kindle and Nook devices are the most popular devices. Kobo is another device that is gaining popularity because it can be used on mobile devices and smartphones. You will likely need to hire someone to format the book, sign up for an account to distribute your e-book, and once it is ready you can have it available in a relatively short amount of time.

Maintaining a Modern Educator Status

A Modern Educator is someone who does more than teach online classes. They are active in the field of education and their chosen subject matter. They know how to teach using technological tools and engage in a virtual community of educators through social media.

The Modern Educator is also conducting research and making intellectual contributions through technological means. The work they publish is done through technologically-enabled resources and made immediately available for their intended audience. They know how to use social media to promote their work and share resources with other educators and students.

It is time now for the Modern Educator mentality to become the standard for online learning. Instruction has adapted in format from traditional to online, and so too must the instructor. It is also important that online schools and hiring specialists recognize the new Modern Educator. This is someone who has likely taught for several institutions because of fluctuating enrollments and staff changes; however, what matters most is their ongoing professional development and intellectual contributions.

The most desirable candidate for an online teaching position is someone with more than extensive work as an online educator. It is someone who can also utilize technological tools as a means of publishing their work and connecting with other educators. A Modern Educator is the new college professor and the one most prepared for teaching through the use of technology.

Advice from a Modern Educator

There was a time not too long ago when online learning was gaining popularity, there were plenty of opportunities available to teach online. But that time has changed, due to the increased number of schools that offer online classes and changes that have occurred in the for-profit or online learning industry.

Potential students have numerous schools to choose from when they want to earn a degree online and there has been a decline in enrollment for some of the for-profit schools because of intense scrutiny by regulators and the student loan crisis. What is needed now more than ever is a realistic overview of online teaching, from someone who has been highly involved in the field as a Modern Educator.

A Perspective about Students

I have been involved in the field of online learning now as a Modern Educator for over ten years. I have taught online courses for traditional colleges as well as for-profit universities. My perspective is not limited to just one school and I have also worked with online faculty development and online curriculum development.

There are a few generalities I can make based upon this experience and the first is about the online student base. With for-profit schools an entrance exam or evaluation of the skill sets that potential students may have (or not have) is generally not used and that means the doors are figuratively wide open. With for-profits they have to compete for new enrollments and as a result they may accept students who are not well-suited for this environment, including those who are academically underprepared. An indicator of the underlying problem for online schools is the retention rate, which is 30% or less on an average for undergraduate programs.

A Perspective about Faculty

Once someone obtains an opportunity as an adjunct there are never any guarantees made about continued employment. You could be a long-term employee and without notice find yourself let go as departmental priorities change. There have been some full-time positions advertised, but those jobs are few and difficult to obtain. Preference may be given to internal employees, leaving current adjuncts to compete with external candidates. There is also an issue of salary. Some full-time positions may require advanced degrees and pay a marginally acceptable rate. Some for-profits also prefer to hire instructors with minimal experience, as a means of keeping the cost of salaries down.

Managing Your Expectations

Since the field of online learning has changed, I want to help manage expectations about online teaching. If you are student now and have little to no teaching experience, and believe you will gain a full-time job right out of school, you have an unrealistic expectation. If you want to teach online because it sounds easy, it may provide steady income, or it would be no different than teaching in a traditional classroom, you will still need to manage and possibly adjust your expectations.

Online teaching requires a significant investment of time if you want to be effective at it, and it requires a specialized skill set to teach in a technologically enable environment. If you want to teach online because you are interested in helping others learn, and you are willing to learn and adapt, you will be more successful if you accept working without any guarantees as an adjunct. The key to successfully teaching online is making a commitment to your ongoing professional development and building a resume that demonstrates your interest in and capacity for online teaching.

Strategies to Build a Career

The following strategies are those that I have implemented and should help you as you work to become a Modern Educator.

Continue Your Professional Development:

Earning a graduate degree is an important step taken for your career. However, as an educator you know the value of ongoing development and the need to keep your knowledge of the subjects you teach current. Your commitment to the field of education means that you need to continually update your skills and strategies.

While some schools have mandatory professional development requirements, you can make it a regular practice. For example, many online associations offer webinars at little or no cost. The point is to stay current in the field of online learning and teaching.

Develop an Engaging Online Presence:

If you are an online educator, you can transform into a Modern Educator. This means you teach online and you can engage with a much broader online academic community. There are several options available for establishing an online presence. LinkedIn allows you to join professional groups. Twitter is a helpful networking resource that allows you to connect with the global academic group and share resources. Whatever options you choose, be certain to carefully manage your image and aware of the digital footprint left behind with everything you post.

Become Published with Articles, a Blog, or E-Books:

The traditional route for a college professor is to conduct research and publish articles in scholarly journals. As a Modern Educator my primary focus is publishing work that can immediately reach other educators and students, and I have done this through a blog, online articles, self-published books, and e-books. I recommend you take the same approach and find a platform to share your knowledge and expertise, whether you offer it for free or you monetize it in some manner.

Develop a Professional CV with Impact:

If you are going to apply for online teaching jobs, you should know there will be strong competition. This means your CV will not only represent you, it needs to provide a clear indication that you are highly qualified. Make certain that it is well-edited, well-formatted, well-written, and demonstrates your commitment to the field of online learning through associations, professional development, and sources of your work as a published author.

Acquire Teaching or Training Experience:

There was a time when a master's degree and a little experience was all someone needed to secure an online teaching job. Now that the number of jobs available are in short supply and the number of applicants as increased, which means every aspect of your background will count.

You will need some experience either in teaching or training and that means you should be on the lookout for those opportunities. I got my start in the field of higher education by teaching at a community college. The purpose is to demonstrate that you have hands-on experience and are capable of teaching adults.

Demand for Modern Educators

I have worked for a variety of institutions that offer online classes. Some offer regular course offerings and others maintain a pool of adjuncts without offering any guarantees. It is understandable that enrollment numbers are going to fluctuate and so too will new teaching assignments. However, the lack of consistency and appreciation for effective and engaging instructors is an ongoing problem for some institutions.

I have been fortunate to work for online schools that value their faculty, including their adjunct instructors. I worked hard to establish myself as a highly engaged instructor. The point of this is that when you are able to gain an adjunct position you want to make certain that you have the time necessary to meet and exceed the facilitation requirements. If you are provided with an opportunity to take on leadership roles, do so as it can help bolster your resume.

Is online teaching a lucrative career? As an adjunct it is possible that over time you will develop more options for your career, especially with ongoing professional development, but you won't always have job security or regular benefits. If you are able to secure a full-time teaching position you will likely gain a better degree of job certainty.

The best advice I can offer is to develop your interest in online teaching as a career strategy and carefully manage the development of your role as a Modern Educator. With time and professional development, you will likely find opportunities. Be sure to manage your expectations and establish a purpose for this type of work as a career choice.

End of Chapter Check-In

What Have You Learned?

What Are Your Strengths?

What Are Your Developmental Areas?

What Will You Apply to Your Teaching Practice?